M000033340

Perspectives – Book 1 – What Does God Want? by Walker James

Copyright © 2014 – 2018 J. Walker Publishing, LLC

Publish by J. Walker Publishing – 600 W. Avenue L Unit 35, Calimesa, CA 92320.

This book is a work of non-fiction. Some names and identifying details have been changed to protect the privacy of individuals.

Note: Unless otherwise noted, all scripture references come from the *Holy Bible, English Standard Version (ESV)*.

Front Cover Design by: Deja vvu/99Designs.com
Back Cover Photo by: Britney Jay
Back Cover content by: Jennifer Stark
Forward by: David and Liza Coldren
Initial Edit by: Darla Partridge at The Write Words Editing Service
Final Edit by: EditorNancy/Fiverr.com

About the Author

Walker James is a Christian author who enjoys writing, teaching, speaking and encouraging others to fall in love with a mighty God, how they can get to know Him, who He is and what He wants.

Walker is an active member of his community church in Southern California where he has served as the small groups coordinator and group leader as well as a drummer on the worship team.

A Christian since the age of 15, Walker has spent years studying the Bible and reading hundreds of books by well-known Christian authors, such as A. W. Tozer, Dallas Willard, Lee Strobel, Norman Geisler, Chuck Swindoll, David Jeremiah and many more.

While learning as much as possible about God and His Beloved Son Jesus from the fantastic pastor, teacher, and author Skip Heitzig, Walker became very passionate about sharing Him with others. He desires to share with you the tremendous value and benefit to you when you enter into a "real" relationship with God.

Walker, a U.S. Marine veteran, lives with his wife Diana in Southern California. Together, they have four children.

To learn more about Walker and the other projects he is involved in, please visit his website at walkerjamesauthor.com.

Foreword

You never know the impact you will have in other people's lives, nor do you too often realize the impact other people will have in your life. My wife, Liza, and I have moved forward spiritually since meeting Walker and attending one of his "Perspectives" classes. What started as a 10-week class at our local church took longer than 4 months to complete, probably due to my constant questions and his simple, but thorough, answers. Questions like:

- Why did God kill all the animals with the flood just because of the bad humans?
- Why does the Old Testament have so many sacrifices, but there are none in the New Testament?
- Which religion should I pick?
- What if I pick the wrong one?
- How many good things do I need to do to get into Heaven?

His answers were uncomplicated and always pointed us back to God. Looking back now, we can see we didn't know God all that well, and because we didn't know Him, we found it easy to judge and possibly condemn some of the things in His Word we didn't like or agree with.

This book isn't about following a bunch of rules, regulations or rituals; it's about walking WITH Jesus. As you move through this series, Walker shows exactly what God wants and why. He lays a foundation that will adequately nurture and support what God wants. He will show you how important questions are, how they help us learn more about God, and how the answers help us fall more in love with Him. He will also guide you into asking God the right questions.

In this book, you will get to see just how beautiful you are to God and how there is nothing you can do to prevent Him from loving you.

What we have learned from Walker has helped us get to know more about God, who He is and what He wants, and this knowledge of God has helped us fall deeper in love with Him. In addition, we have come to understand and value God's Word tremendously, which has helped us to engage in good, loving conversations with those in need.

You do not need to quote scriptures like a pastor, but the Word of God is your only offensive weapon in your battle against God's enemies. May the sword of the Spirit protect you. Clash! Bang! Jesus wins!

We would like to encourage you to take this journey with Walker. Find out what God wants. Learn more about Him. Fall in love with Him as we have.

Let Jesus be your defense attorney on your final day of judgment with God. Have a relationship with Jesus so He can defend you and claim that He knows you and that you belong to Him. Move forward each day with Jesus and see how your life and those around you can change in a positive direction.

Our highest gratitude to you, Walker, for being such a guide in our spiritual journey and answering all those tough questions we threw at you every week. God bless you. We love you.

David and Liza Coldren

Dedication

To my Lord and my God, words fail to express the gratitude I have in the deepest parts of my soul for the love and patience you have had with me and for me. Thank you! ♡

Table of Contents

One: Perspective

"What are you doing to me?" I screamed, shaking my fist at God and sobbing. "Who do you think you are? What have I ever done to deserve this from you? How dare you destroy my life!" Obviously, I wasn't finished unleashing my anger and rage at a God. "And You say You love me—what a joke!" I quipped, stomping off in a rage.

How do you know God loves you? Just because some people say He does, does that prove that He does? What if tragedy strikes your life? Does He still love you then? What if lightning strikes twice? What if when this disaster strikes, He ignores your pleas for answers? Then what if He ignores your demands for answers? Does He love you then? What if you get angry at Him and throw a 12-year temper tantrum saying, "Ok, if you are not going to talk to me, well then I am NOT going to talk to you!"

This tragedy was the beginning of one of the hardest challenges of my life. Anyone who has been tested by God in this fashion can tell you this is not an easy test to endure, let alone pass, especially when a trial like this begins after you've been His disciple and His child for almost eight years. You may even ask yourself, "What kind of cruel game is God playing with me?"

Would it surprise you to know that in my anger, in my rage, I misjudged God? I had an incorrect perspective of Him and of what He was doing in my life and what He ultimately wanted from me. Worse yet, I refused to look at my situation from His perspective. After all, it was rather easy to do considering I could only see things from "my" perspective, not His. Let me clarify, I "chose" to see things only from "my" perspective. I did not care about "His" perspective, at all.

From my perspective, God was punishing me, God was judging me, God was picking on me. For what? Some sin I may have committed? What kind of sin could I have committed that would have been worthy of this retaliatory punishment—this devastation and outright destruction to my hopes and dreams?

Imagine with me for a second. What if I were to take a step back and try to see my life from His perspective? What would that tell me about Him? What would that tell me about His love for me? Are these trials, tribulations, and struggles I'm going through His fault or mine? Have I played a "role" in the events of my life? Have I made the choices that resulted in the challenges, or has He imposed them on me? Is He just picking on me because He is bored and has nothing better to do? Am I that important that He would go out of His way to purposefully cause me this much anguish, this much heartache, this much pain? How much was His fault and how much was my fault? Is that even the right question I should be asking? Does blaming God give me the satisfaction I seek? Or is it just another dead-end?

Here is where perspective comes in. A *perspective* is a point-of-view. It's a way of looking at something, implying you can look at something in more than one way. Let me give you a humorous example:

> An artist, a preacher, and a cowboy all come up to the Grand Canyon at the same time. The artist looks out and says: "Oh my, what a magnificent painting for me to paint." The preacher looks out and says: "Amen! What an amazing display of God's ga-lory." The cowboy takes a long hard look and shaking his head says: "I don't know about y'all, but THAT would be one horrible place to lose a cow!"

These three people were all looking at the same thing, the Grand Canyon, yet they each had a different perspective on what they saw. I too have had this problem, looking at God and not seeing Him and what He's doing correctly, but instead, viewing my life and my struggles through my flawed eyesight, blaming Him for all the tragedies and problems I found therein.

Whether we admit it or not, we all have a perspective of God—who He is, what He's like, and what He wants, even if that perspective says, there is no God. The only problem with billions of perspectives of God is they can't all be right. What can we do? Do we give up on knowing God? Does knowing God become a futile endeavor? A waste of time? Is He even knowable? How do we even get to an ultimate point of knowing what He wants if we can't seem to get to know Him?

The first thing we need to do is agree that someone else's perspective of God, although it may be relevant to them and may have some value, is not what's important. Your perspective of God is irrelevant compared to God's perspective of Himself!

Perspective #1: Your perspective of God is irrelevant compared to God's perspective of Himself!

What you, me or someone else thinks about God may indeed be of value, but in the end, it does not matter. The only thing that matters is what God says about Himself, period, end of the sentence! After all, the ONLY perspective of God we can trust is God's view of Himself!

Wouldn't it be nice if we had a book or a manual that would tell us about God and give us a glimpse of what He is like and what He wants? Maybe even show us just how much He loves us? Show us the depth of His love for us? How He would pay the highest price He could to redeem us. There is such a book, or should I say a series of letters compiled into one book: the Bible.

This book is essential as it gives us God's perspective of Himself. Now, before you get mad and come up with some excuse about how it can't be trusted, how it was written by men or some other reason for discounting the Bible, let me encourage you to set those arguments aside for just a second. I will address them, but not right now. Right now, we need to focus on the question at hand, "How do we get God's perspective of Himself?"

The Bible is one of the tools we can use to do this. However, before we can dive into that too deep, there are a few more things we need to learn first.

Learning God's perspective of Himself allows us to establish a rule for our life. If our view or someone else's view of God does not agree with God's perspective of Himself, we can throw it away as garbage, as a lie. After all, who knows more about God than God Himself? With that said, it makes sense for us to adopt His perspective of Himself. When we do, it ensures that we maintain His viewpoint and not someone else's.

The next logical question would be, is God knowable? Can we know Him?

Towards the end of His sermon on the mount, Jesus took the time to answer this question directly when He said:

> *Ask, and it will be given to you; seek, and you will find; knock, and it will be opened to you. For everyone who asks receives, and the one who seeks finds, and to the one who knocks it will be opened. – Matthew 7:7-8*

The perspective Jesus is putting forth here is, if you put in the effort, if you sincerely ask, if you sincerely seek and if you sincerely knock, God will become knowable to you. Understand, knowing God requires effort; it requires work. The question will always be: Are you willing to put in the effort? Are you willing to put in the work? Are you willing to ask? Are you willing to seek? Are you willing to knock?

This series of books are designed to take you through the natural progression of knowing God and getting to know Him in a more profound, more personal way. My goal is to try to help as many people avoid the pitfalls and struggles I fell into while getting to know God and what He wants.

This project started in October 2014 as a single book that God transformed into a series of books. What I found out as I got into writing, and then into teaching the content, was something my good friend Mike Bagg reminded me of. He said, "Take your time. One thing I've learned, when you are teaching others to fall in love with God, you can't rush it. We have a BIG God, and it takes time, effort and work to get to know Him." Which means, we should be patient; God's Word is essential to getting to know Him. Do not skip it, and do not ignore it. Respect it, and it will teach you great and wonderful things about Him!

It is my prayer that this series will appeal to those who know a lot about God, those who don't know anything about Him, and everyone in between. I'm not a theologian; I'm just a guy who has fallen in love with an amazing God and wanted you to know just how much He loves you personally.

Regardless of who you are, your age, gender, race, nationality, religion, background, education, secrets, crimes, or sins, we are all the same in God's eyes. Before God, every single one of us is His child, He has NO grandchildren, which means we are all on the same footing. There is no difference between you and me, none, nada, zero, zilch! We all have the equal opportunity to ask, seek and knock. Some of us will ask a little, some of us will ask a lot, and some won't ask at all. However, that has more to do with effort than position.

This series is laid out and designed to be a step-by-step guide through the journey of getting to know God and what He wants. Since one of my greatest problems was not knowing much about Him, and then sadly misjudging Him when tragedy struck my life, I want to make sure others don't fall into the trap I did. You see, the more we know about God, the better we will be able to look at our lives from His perspective.

Understand, it has taken me a lifetime for God to grow me and get me to where I am today, and believe me, I am still a work in progress. That is what is so remarkable about God—your relationship with God is a journey. Over time, as you partner with Him and cooperate with Him, He molds and shapes you into a beautiful reflection of His Son Jesus Christ.

Perspective #3: Your relationship with God is a journey. Over time, as you partner with Him and cooperate with Him, He molds and shapes you into a beautiful reflection of His Son Jesus Christ.

Granted, the more you cooperate with Him, the faster these changes can occur. One of the purposes of this series is to present you with the perspectives I've learned from God and from many others. These were not easy perspectives to learn, especially for a rebellious, uncooperative child such as myself, but they are valuable reminders and a way of looking at our lives that will help us focus on what is essential.

Perspective is a choice. What perspective you use to see God is also a choice. What perspective you choose to see God working in your life, again, is a choice. Let me encourage you to learn what God's view of Himself is, and what He wants. Then look at your life from "His" perspective! In the end, what perspective you choose will always be up to you, so *choose wisely*!

Perspective Recap:

- **Perspective #1**: Your perspective of God is irrelevant compared to God's perspective of Himself!
- **Perspective #2:** Be patient. God's Word is essential to getting to know Him. Do not skip it, and do not ignore it. Respect it, and it will teach you great and wonderful things about Him!
- **Perspective #3:** Your relationship with God is a journey. Over time as you partner with Him and cooperate with Him, He molds and shapes you into a beautiful reflection of His Son Jesus Christ.

Two: My Story

January 29, 1983, was the day my oldest son, Joshua, was born. It was 12:05 AM and I was exhausted and excited. As a brand-new father, I was young and had dreams of how I was going to teach my son to play baseball, football, basketball, and golf. He was going to be a superstar! I just knew it! One day, I would be sitting in the stands watching him play, cheering him on, and after he scored his one-millionth touchdown in a game, I would say, "Yep, that's MY boy! Taught him everything he knows!" Of course, he would turn to the cameras and say, "Hi, Mom!" but, I was okay with that. Even though my son hadn't done anything yet, I was proud of him and all the things he would grow up to do.

I was surprised and quite frankly caught off guard by the depth and the amount of love I had for this little guy I was holding in my arms for the first time. I remember thinking, "I'm his father, and I'm responsible for him. Oh, how I love him. He is my son!"

To be honest, I didn't know you could love someone you just met so profoundly, so quickly. That was the way it was with him. I knew the day he was born that he was special, and he was going to change my life. I just didn't know then how accurate of a statement that would prove to be.

Joshua and I did everything together. When it was time for him to take a nap, he slept on my chest. I didn't have a problem changing his diapers, feeding him or playing with him. I loved being a father, especially being his father. We would laugh together, play together. He quickly became my world, and he was so much fun to have around. I found out he was pretty flexible too. I could bend him in half and tickle him, and he would just giggle, begging me with his laugh for more.

When Joshua was five months old, we suspected something was wrong with him. Physically, he looked perfectly healthy; he just wasn't doing some of the things you'd expect a five-month-old baby to do, like sit up, roll over, or start to crawl.

At eight months, Joshua was diagnosed with "mixed cerebral palsy." Bottom line: he would be a quadriplegic for the rest of his life. He would never crawl, never walk, never run, and never talk, ever! Never learn how to play sports, never learn how to drive a car, never fall in love, never get married, never have children of his own, never say "Hey, Dad, I love you."

I was devastated. My initial response was, "Well, God must know what He's doing. He must think we can handle this challenge." I'm not sure if I believed that or whether I felt that was the thing to say at a time like this.

The doctors told us they did not normally see cerebral palsy as a birth defect. Typically, it was caused by head trauma or a traumatic brain injury, like lack of oxygen during birth, a car accident, falling off a bike, or being thrown from a horse. They also said that CP, as it's called, as a birth-defect, was extremely rare, the odds being something like nine million-to-one. They said we could have more children and they would be perfectly healthy, so we were hopeful. Sure, I was sad for my son, Joshua, but my dreams for a superstar were still alive, or so I thought.

After Joshua had been diagnosed, nothing changed. He was still my son. I was hopelessly in love with him; he was beautiful and precious. He was everything to me, and he was still exceptional. To be honest, at the time, I didn't know I needed him so much. He was still a baby, so the impact of caring for a child with special needs would not take full effect for another year or so.

If you have never had a child with special needs, it's hard to comprehend the burden. It's having to care for someone else 24/7. They never learn to care for themselves. You must change their diapers. You must feed them. You must dress them. You must lift them and carry them everywhere you go. When they are hurt or sick, you can try to comfort them, but you never really know whether you are getting through or not. You never really know if they understand what you are saying. And this burden magnifies every year. They continue to grow, get taller, get heavier, and you don't ever seem to get a break. No one understands your burden, your heartache, your disappointment, your pain or your crushed dreams. No one seems to be able to comfort you and help you feel it is going to be ok. You feel desperately alone and forsaken.

Somehow, I'm not sure how you move forward. As time goes on, the burden becomes more and more challenging, but somehow, you get stronger, you get used to the burden, you manage, you find a way to survive. You avoid things that are too difficult, and you do things that are a bit easier. You find short-cuts. The heartache, disappointment, and pain lessen; however, they never go away. You want answers, and there are none to be found. You ask God why, but He just ignores you as if He doesn't care.

About 11 months after we found out how "special" Joshua was, my second son Matthew arrived. Like his brother, he looked perfectly normal. There were no problems with the birth, and he seemed perfectly healthy.

Right away, Matthew "seemed" different than his brother Joshua. He "felt" healthy and not disabled. I'm not sure how much of that was wishful thinking and how much of that was true. However, when Matthew was five months old, we knew, beyond a shadow of a doubt, that he, like his brother, had been born with mixed cerebral palsy and would also be a quadriplegic for the rest of his life as well.

Two sons, brothers, both born with mixed cerebral palsy. I'd like to say my response to this second challenge was as noble as the first. However, that would be a lie.

Now I was mad. Mad at God. Shaking my fist at Him, I said, "Who do you think you are? What are you trying to do to me? What have I ever done to deserve this from you? Why are YOU picking on me?" Even, "How dare you rob me of all my dreams!" (Of course, I said this in the snottiest, nastiest tone I could muster.)

I know I was harsh, angry, and pretty much a jerk. I wanted answers from God. Unfortunately, I did not get any answers; I only got silence.

If you know anything about God, He rarely feels the need to explain Himself and what He does. Consequently, and at times, talking to Him was like talking to a brick wall, and everything was bouncing off.

I showed Him though. If He was not going to talk to me and give me the answers I demanded, then I wasn't going to speak to Him either.

Stubbornly, I stayed mad at God for 12 years. Oh sure, I believed in Him. After all, I became a disciple of Jesus Christ when I was 15 years old. Nevertheless, God wasn't doing a good job of cooperating with me and my plans, so I figured I had a right to be mad at Him. Then again, I was more than mad; I was furious at how He had ruined my life. How He had given me not one but two boys with special needs. How was I ever going to deal with this burden?

Understand, I've never held the fact that my two boys had special needs against them. In His infinite wisdom, God took the brunt of my wrath for this fact. In short, God protected them by allowing me to vent my anger and frustration on Him. My boys have always been very precious and special to me. Oh sure, I've gotten upset at them when they are all dressed, in their wheelchairs and ready for school, and the school bus comes to pick them up, and one of them throws up all over himself. And then I had to take him out of his wheelchair, clean him and the wheelchair up, get him dressed again, put him back into his wheelchair and drive him to school and try not to be late for work. One morning, it would be one son, the next morning it would be the other. In fact, some mornings it would be both. Honestly, I'm not sure how I survived.

On occasion, I would talk to God if I was in a bind and needed something. If He didn't respond the way I thought He should, I just chalked it up to Him hating on me some more. I guess He had nothing better to do then to pick on poor little me.

Come to think of it, I was rude and obnoxious to Him. I'm not sure why He didn't send a bolt of lightning or two my way. I most certainly deserved them.

Now, imagine my shame when I finally woke up after being angry at God for 12 years and realized God was never "picking" on me; He was protecting me, loving me, blessing me. I was just too stubborn to see it.

You see, I have never had to worry about my boys getting bad grades in school, getting into fights, shoplifting, getting drunk then driving a car and possibly killing someone, getting addicted to drugs and living on the street, robbing, stealing, or hurting other people.

No, my boys only know how to do one thing, and that is love. Anyone who comes near them, they will love. They will smile, they will laugh, and they will do their best to play with them.

You see, "perspective."

The bad news? My perspective of God and what He was doing in my life was all wrong. I refused to see Him for who He was and what He was trying to do. In fact, for 12 years, I wallowed in self-pity thinking, "I am a victim, God hates me, God is picking on me, poor me!"

The good news? God was patient with me. Why, I do not know. Somehow, He opened my eyes to see what I was missing, to show me just how much He loved me, to help me understand and appreciate how truly blessed I am. To finally start seeing my life from His perspective.

What did I learn?

My 12-year temper tantrum at God accomplished two things. First, it showed me how much God loved me. I finally saw how much God was protecting me and how precious and valuable I was to God. After all, I could have been a nervous wreck, worrying about all the harmful things in this world my children could be doing. Instead, all I had to worry about was who they were going to love on next. Such a burden!

My problem was, even though I had been a disciple of Jesus Christ for almost eight years when tragedy struck, I didn't have the slightest clue as to who God was, let alone what He wanted. Therefore, I was ill-equipped, when tested, to respond properly.

Bottom line, I did not know God. This started a burning question inside me: "If I am struggling to know God and who He is, there must be others suffering from the same problem." Why is it so hard to get to know God and what He wants in the first place? I'm sure He would have more followers if He made it a little easier, right?

It is easy; it doesn't behoove God to make it hard or complicated. It does, however, require effort on our part. It must be something we "want" to be. We must be curious; we can't just ask the tough questions and run when we don't get an answer we like. We need to stick around and invest the time it takes to understand and accept the tough answers.

Probably the most important thing I have learned from all this is we must have a better perspective of who God is. Instead of asking Him WHY or asking Him to explain or defend Himself and what He in His wisdom has either done or allowed, I needed to change my perspective and my questions and ask God:

- What are You trying to teach me in this?
- What is it You want me to learn?
- How do You want me to respond to this?
- How can I shine Your light, Your love, and Your Son Jesus in and through this?
- How can I serve and glorify You in this?
- How can I use this to help me fall more in love with You?

By doing this, I changed my perspective from demanding answers from God to one of asking God how I could cooperate with Him and what He was doing. God doesn't have to defend Himself, especially to you. After all, He is God, and well, you are not.

Perspective #4: God doesn't have to defend Himself, especially to you. After all, He is God and you are not.

It is important for us to understand, asking God the WHY question is usually asking for the silent treatment. Because He is God, He doesn't owe anyone an answer to WHY!

Perspective #5: Asking God the WHY question is usually asking for the silent treatment. Because He is God, He doesn't owe anyone an answer to WHY!

Now, if you ask Him WHAT He wants you to learn and HOW you can cooperate with Him, He loves responding and answering these questions. When you do this, you begin to cooperate with God and understand EVERYTHING that comes into your life must FIRST go through the hands of God.

Perspective #6: "EVERYTHING that comes into your life must FIRST go through the hands of God."
– Greg Laurie

If we recognize this to be true, then everything we are going through has been APPROVED by God for whatever purpose or reason He may have. Even if He chooses to give you not one but two boys with special needs.

You see, God sees our lives from beginning to end, not just in this moment we see. He sees everything. Which means He knows exactly what we are going to need today to help us better serve Him and His kingdom tomorrow.

I've heard it said, "Don't waste the pain." God allowed the pain to come into your life for a reason. Ask Him to show you how to benefit from it, to learn from it, to grow from it.

God is patient, extremely patient, with us. God loves us dearly, more than we may ever know, realize, comprehend or understand. Bottom line, we need to use everything that God allows into our lives to draw us closer to Him, to help us fall more in love with Him, and to become the person God wants us to be.

You see, "perspective."

Where did I go wrong? How did I make such a big mistake, such a big miscalculation, thinking God was one thing when He was something entirely different?

If I'm honest, it was because I didn't know God. For that matter, I had never taken the time to get to know him, who He was or what He wanted. As I said, I became a disciple of Jesus Christ when I was 15 years old, which means I thought I knew him for seven and a half years, before my first son was born, before tragedy struck. Before I was "tested!" Shouldn't I have known better? Shouldn't I have been able to trust in Him and what He was doing?

I'm sure many people are or have been mad at God, or are staying mad at Him for years. This shows they do not know Him, nor do they understand what He, in His wisdom, is doing and why. They refuse to see who He is or to try to understand His point-of-view, His perspective. Instead of pursuing Him, we get mad or angry at Him and at what He is doing. We are deeply hurt by what is happening in our lives. We want answers and become frustrated when our questions go unanswered, feeling we are being "ignored" by Him!

Our problem isn't so much with what He has or has not done. Our problem is we often don't know or understand the why He's doing or allowing the things we are experiencing. We fail to get the why answered. The reason for this is because we don't know Him. If we knew Him, we could match up the things we are going through with who we know Him to be. That is the moment we gain clarity and perspective of Him. When we know that He is loving, kind and generous beyond our wildest dreams, we know that this trial, this struggle is not meant to hurt us. Instead, it is intended to grow us. Why? So, we can come alongside one another and partner with God to help each other with the same or similar challenges. If we never take the time to learn from our trials, how can God get any value out of them and use us to give the lesson and the love to someone else?

Perspective #7: If we never take the time to learn from our trials, how can God get any value out of them and use us to give the lesson and the love to someone else?

When we are going through something traumatic, something that feels so devastating we can't stand it, we are unsure how we are going to get through it. That is when we need God most. That is when we could use a friend to come alongside us and hug us and remind us to lean on who we know God to be. And if we don't know Him very well, then they can encourage us to invest the time to get to know Him better.

When we know the truth about God, who He is and what He wants, our relationship with Him deepens. It grows and blossoms into a light that touches and infects so many other lives. Sure, He gets the glory, but you get to help!

One of the pastors I listen to quite often and consider a mentor, Skip Heitzig, tells a great story that illustrates the point I'm trying to make:

One day, he (Skip) was building a fence and his son Nathan (who I think was only 4 or 5 at the time) asked if he could help. Skip didn't want the help; he knew he could get the job done faster without him. However, because he wanted to spend time with his son, he said sure. He gave him a little hammer and some nails and showed his son how to hold the board and how to hammer the nails. Of course, he would correct any mistakes his son made during the process without his son even noticing.

Finally, they were finished, and mom (Lenya) came out to inspect. Nathan said to his mom, "Look, Mom, what do you think of the fence Dad and I built?"

Of course, Nathan didn't do too much of the work, but he took most of the credit.

When we get to heaven and start telling stories, I think a lot of them are going to be just like this one: "Look at the fence God and I built." I'm glad everyone will know that God let me help Him, and He showed me how to hammer the nails, and he would fix and straighten the mistakes I made without me even knowing it. All because He wanted to spend some time with me! Knowing that God wants to spend time with us should encourage us to want to spend time with Him.

Perspective #8: Knowing that God wants to spend time with us should encourage us to want to spend time with Him!

When we know God, we can better understand what He's doing in our lives. If we know Him and what He's doing, if we look at our lives from His perspective, we can then cooperate with Him, partner with Him and His plan for His Kingdom rather than getting in His way.

Perspective #9: When we look at our lives from God's perspective, we can then cooperate with Him, partner with Him and His plan for His Kingdom!

One thing I am learning to do is to help others find out what God wants and to help them leverage that perspective into a fuller, happier life. A life where they are partnering with God, cooperating with Him and what He is doing instead of fighting Him like I was. A life full of happiness and joy, even when things do not go their way, rather than a life full of anger, bitterness, and hatred, shaking their fist at God and what He's doing or allowing to occur in their life. A life of being mad at the world, the creator of it, and everyone in it. We need to understand that just because things are not going the way we planned doesn't mean they are not going the way they should!

Perspective #10: Just because things are not going the way we planned doesn't mean they are not going the way they should! – Christine Caine

---

Here is where your perspective has a direct impact on the depth and quality of your life. Choose a negative perspective and get negative results. Choose a positive perspective and get positive results. The choice of perspective will always be yours to make.

Perspective #11: Your perspective has a direct impact on the depth and quality of your life. Choose a negative perspective and get negative results. Choose a positive perspective and get positive results.

When you choose to see God as a cosmic bully, you continue to fight against Him, as I did. When you choose to look at God as someone who loves you profoundly and cares about you personally, you find out what a joy He is and what blessings He has in store for you, even when you are being tested. His joy does not leave you because He has promised:

Be strong and courageous. Do not fear or be in dread of them, for it is the Lord your God who goes with you. He will not leave you or forsake you. – Deuteronomy 31:6

God is faithful. God keeps ALL His promises. God is with you always; He will NEVER leave you. He will NEVER forsake you. EVER! You may choose to forsake Him, but he will never forsake you! That is what God's love does. He cares for you, even when you don't care for Him.

Perspective #12: That is what God's love does! He cares for you even when you don't care for Him.

The one thing I've often overlooked is how my perspective of God—who He is and what He wants—has a direct impact on my perspective. The more I get to know Him, and this is a lifelong process, the more I fall in love with Him. The more I fall in love with Him, the more of Him I want to get to know. And that, my friend, is a good thing!

Perspective Recap:

- **Perspective #4:** God doesn't have to defend Himself, especially to you. After all, He is God and you are not.
- **Perspective #5:** Asking God the WHY question is usually asking for the silent treatment. Because He is God, He doesn't owe anyone an answer to WHY!
- **Perspective #6:** "EVERYTHING that comes into your life must FIRST go through the hands of God." – Greg Laurie
- **Perspective #7:** If we never take the time to learn from our trials, how can God get any value out of them and use us to give the lesson and the love to someone else?
- **Perspective #8:** Knowing that God wants to spend time with us should encourage us to want to spend time with Him!
- **Perspective #9:** When we look at our lives from God's perspective, we can then cooperate with Him, partner with Him and His plan for His Kingdom!
- **Perspective #10:** Just because things are not going the way we planned doesn't mean they are not going the way they should! – Christine Caine
- **Perspective #11:** Your perspective has a direct impact on the depth and quality of your life. Choose a negative perspective and get negative results. Choose a positive perspective and get positive results.
- **Perspective #12:** That is what God's love does! He cares for you even when you don't care for Him!

Three: Evidence

In a court trial, you can pronounce someone guilty based on the preponderance of the evidence. You do not need proof. Although proof is always nice to have, it is not necessary to pronounce someone guilty or innocent of a crime. Likewise, proving the existence of God can be done considering the preponderance of the evidence; it doesn't require overwhelming proof. The question that only you can answer is, how much evidence will it take for you to believe that God does indeed exist? That God does indeed love and care for you deeply?

Perspective #13: How much evidence will it take for you to believe that God does indeed exist? That God does indeed love and care for you deeply?

Some people have an open mind. They are curious about God and what He wants, and they are not necessarily afraid to be accountable to Him. Because they invest the time it takes to get to know Him, they are free to gain a better perspective of Him and of His Kingdom. To this kind of person, the truth is what is essential, so they eagerly seek the truth, understanding that sometimes the truth can be hard to find and hard to uncover.

Perspective #14: Truth can be hard to find and hard to uncover.

However, it is always important to understand that truth will always reward the diligent who sincerely seek after her and are not afraid of her.

Perspective #15: Truth will always reward the diligent who sincerely seek after her and are not afraid of her.

For others, evidence for the existence of God must be ignored or dismissed at any cost, even when the evidence is undeniable or overwhelming. The only legitimate reason I can come up with for this is that they are afraid of the truth. These skeptics and critics are usually close-minded and are biased to their position, refusing to believe, discuss, or listen to anything that does not support their position.

Thus, the truth scares them. Since they do not want to be accountable to the truth, they ignore it, cast doubt on it, or plainly just do not believe it, no matter how compelling the evidence may be. It is a question of their will to not accept the truth. This becomes most evident when it comes to accepting the truth of God's existence.

These people typically prefer another less plausible explanation that has nothing to do with God. The reason for this may be caused by some great hurt or pain in their life they are blaming God for. Or they just do not want to be accountable to God. Or they see God as a crutch, something meant only for the weak. This perspective forces them to ignore anything and everything implying or referring to God. They choose to discount or dismiss the evidence of God at all costs.

When this is the case, evidence and proof do not matter, because this type of person doesn't want to believe. They may say it is because there is not enough evidence, or there is still some doubt. Nevertheless, this is seldom the actual reason. The real reason is they do not want to be accountable to God. They want to do their own thing, whatever that may be. Their will says no, and their mind gives excuses.

Or possibly, other so-called "God followers" have mis-represented God, who He is and what He wants for them, causing them to be repelled or repulsed by the idea of God. Unfortunately, God gets blamed for the actions of those who say they follow Him, regardless of whether their actions prove what their words say.

Let me give you an example of what this looks like. Let's say you and I are acquaintances. We are not really friends, but we know of each other. Now, what would happen if I borrowed your car, without your permission of course, and drove it to a nearby shopping mall. I want to do some window shopping, but I really don't feel like getting out of the car, so I just drive through the big mall doors. I might or might not care about all the people in my way, after all "I'm shopping," and they are in MY way! I cruise around the inside of the mall, not caring what I run over or who I run over, causing millions of dollars' worth of damage.

When the police finally stop me, and come to the aid of all those shoppers, I tell the police that YOU told me to do this for you. That it was YOUR idea and it was what YOU wanted. Now, should the police "believe" me and arrest you and make you pay for all the damage and destruction I caused?

Probably not. Yet, so many people blame God for what others have done in His name. In fact, they don't give it a second thought, and yet, if someone was to do that to them, they would be outraged. This of course happens because we don't know God and we've never taken the time to get to know Him. You see, if someone says they are a "God follower" and then they do something God would not do, you can see it from a mile away. Why? Because you know God, and what they did has nothing to do with who God is or what He's like.

However, no matter the reason, no matter the excuse, God will hold you accountable for all the evidence of His existence, regardless of whether you believe it or not.

Perspective #16: God will hold you accountable for all the evidence of His existence, regardless of whether you believe it or not.

Notice this perspective says YOU! It is vital that you understand that regardless of whether you "believe" the evidence or not, God is still going to hold you accountable for the evidence, as it has been there all along and you either choose to believe it or not. The choice will always be your own. You see, God has given us all the power to choose, which means we're in charge. Likewise, this means we are also accountable for the choices we make.

---

*For what can be known about God is plain to them, because God has shown it to them. For his invisible attributes, namely, his eternal power and divine nature, have been clearly perceived, ever since the creation of the world,[1] in the things that have been made. **So they***

---

[1] Or clearly perceived from the creation of the world.

Evidence for the existence of God is everywhere, and it is easy to see because God has intentionally made it easy. If you can't see it, or you refuse to see it, then you are exercising your God-given power to choose, which is perfectly okay. There is absolutely nothing wrong with that, just know that God will hold you and only you accountable for what you choose or do not choose to believe in, including Him.

Proof, on the other hand, is fact that is indisputable. Just like with evidence, there are still a lot of people who choose not to believe the proof even when it is slapping them in the face. For example, Jesus came to earth as the Son of God and did many miracles. He healed the sick, lame and blind; casted out demons; and raised the dead. Most of the people of His day did not believe He was who He said He was. In fact, they regularly wanted to stone Him for making Himself out to be God. They refused to believe even though they saw all the proof. Why is that?

I wasn't there, so I do not know for sure. However, I can surmise their reason is probably similar to the reason most people have today. If they accepted Jesus for who He said He was, then they are accountable to Him and His teachings. And if we are honest, most people do not want to be accountable to anyone, let alone Jesus or God. There seems to be a general perspective that God is just a bunch of rules, regulations, and rituals. Just another burden to carry around, and honestly, who needs or wants another burden?

Of course, that is a misguided perspective on who and what God is. However, before we get to that point, I want to address another. If God does indeed exist, then why doesn't He just provide us with overwhelming proof and remove all doubt?

Before I answer that question, let me ask you a couple more questions. What proof do you require to believe that God exists? Do you need Him to turn water into wine? Do you need to see that He can walk on water? Do you need to see that He can heal the sick? The lame? The blind? The leper? Do you need to see Him cast out demons? Do you need to see Him feed over 5,000 people with just five loaves of bread and two fish? Do you need to see Him raise the dead? Do you need to see Him raise Himself from the dead? How many tricks will it take for you to believe?

Jesus had this same problem. The people of His day saw these signs and more, yet very few of them believed in who He said He was. At the time of His crucifixion, Jesus only had about 120 followers. Considering that He spent over three years walking around Israel teaching, healing the sick, the lame, and the blind, and casting out demons. On one occasion, he fed 5,000 men (15,000 men, women and children) and at another time, he fed 4,000 men (12,000 men, women and children), so why did He only have 120 followers?

That is because God created us with the power to choose. Like I said earlier, with that power, we can have proof slap us in the face but still choose to ignore it. We are free to choose whether we believe the evidence or not. Humans are very clever; most of the time we can come up with a reason or an excuse to not believe the evidence and justify our choice not to believe. Understand, regardless of the choice we make, the reasons for the choice, or how we try to justify the choice, God will still hold us personally accountable!

Let's look at this from God's perspective for a second. You have created humanity, and you have chosen to love them. In return, you want them to love you as well. However, for their love for you to be real, they must be free to choose; their love must be given freely. Which also means, they must be free NOT to choose to love you.

Now, you could put some overwhelming proof out there that they would see and be unable to deny unless they are brain-dead, but that would be like forcing them to love you. Forced love is a contradiction. Forced love would remove the ability to make a conscious choice to love God and to serve Him only. I think this is the primary reason why God has put so much evidence out there for His existence. He wants to make a choice easy for you. He's not into making this hard, but He is all about you having the power and the freedom to make up your mind.

Like I've said several times now, you and only you are accountable for what YOU choose to believe. Let me give you an example of this. Let's say someone you trust, a pastor or a good friend, tells you something about God that is untrue, and you believe it without verifying or investigating it yourself. God is going to hold you accountable for what you believe. True, He may also punish them for spreading the lie, but He will hold you accountable for believing the lie and for not putting forth the effort to validate it. Likewise, if someone tells you, "There is no God," and you believe it without putting any effort into proving it as true, God is still going to hold only you accountable.

Now, given all this, can we prove beyond a shadow of a doubt there either is or is not a God?

NO! It is not possible for us to prove beyond a shadow of a doubt that there is a God. However, we cannot disprove it either. The thing we need to understand is that the finite (limited) cannot prove or disprove the existence of the infinite (unlimited).

Perspective #17: "The finite (limited) cannot prove or disprove the existence of the infinite (unlimited)." – Skip Heitzig

---

The finite has limits, it has boundaries, while the infinite has no boundaries, no limitations. The infinite is unlimited and can do anything, be anything, go anywhere without limits. Roy A. Varghese makes an interesting observation about this fact in his book *The Wonder of the World: A Journey from Modern Science to the Mind of God,* when he says:

> Once you understand what is meant by the concept of God, you understand immediately that the Infinite is not something you can see physically. In order for you to see something physically, it must have shape and size and color. It must reflect light and work its way through our sensory channels until it is registered in the brain. But if you apply these attributes to any being then it can no longer be thought of as infinite. Consequently, we cannot seriously expect God's face to appear on a hillside. And if the words 'I exist, signed God' were to suddenly appear in the sky, this would not prove anything one way or

another since there is no way to verify the source of the message.

Now, how can you put all the knowledge of an infinite being into the mind of a finite being? This, of course, is impossible. Then how do we get to know the infinite? The only way He's chosen to reveal Himself to us is through His "written" Word, the Bible, and His "revealed" Word, His Son Jesus Christ.

We have the evidence. The question then becomes, is there enough evidence to prove the existence of God? The answer to this question is an overwhelming YES! There is more than enough evidence to prove the existence of God. All we need to do is consider the evidence that God has left behind for His existence and then make our choice based on the evidence.

Some people may still choose to say, "I need to see God before I will ever believe in Him." They want a physical experience, not a bunch of evidence. They want to see, feel, taste, touch or hear something to know that He is real.

The only problem with that kind of logic is that just because you do not see, feel, taste, touch or hear something doesn't make it less real. It doesn't mean it doesn't exist. For example, do you have a mind? I do not see it. I can't feel it. I can't taste it. I can't touch it. I do not hear it. So, obviously, you must not have a mind!

Do you see how flawed that logic can be? You have a mind because you are reading this book, and you think, reason, problem solve, create, design and so much more, all with your mind.

There is a ton of evidence to support the fact that you have a mind. However, I still do not physically see it. Just because I do not see it does not make it any less real; it is there. I can see the evidence that you have a mind by how you use it, the things you do with it, and the choices you make with it. Just because you can't see God doesn't mean He doesn't exist.

Proving the existence of God is very similar to determining you have a mind. All we need to do is look at the evidence. Since this is the case, what evidence is required to determine God exists? How about design? If something has design, it must have a designer.

For example, you are digging in your backyard, and suddenly you find a clay pot. You carefully dig it up, clean it off and you notice it has writings on it, some words and pictures. Its shape looks like it was made for carrying water or wine and it has a lid on it to keep its contents inside.

In observing this clay pot, do you say, "Well, I suppose that after billions of years, the dirt in the ground merged with the sand, a few rocks, and some water and then formed this clay pot in this particular shape with a lid. Then over the next several million years, some worms and bugs came along and crawled across the surface of the clay pot and wrote on it and drew the pictures."

Probably not. That's a pretty far-fetched story. It is evident by its "design" that someone created the clay pot, wrote on it and fashioned a lid for it. You do not know who designed it or created it, but you do know someone did. The evidence points to a designer.

Proving God exists is no different, all you need is evidence. Now, what evidence do we have for the existence of God?

Surprisingly, there is a lot of evidence, so much so that I could overwhelm you with evidence that would have your head spinning and you reading for years. However, I do not want to do that; I want to keep it simple. Besides, there are other books out there like Lee Strobel's *Case for a Creator* and Norm Geisler's and Frank Turek's book *I Don't Have Enough Faith to Be an Atheist* that do a much better job of this than I can do.

However, there is one very compelling fact or piece of evidence that points to a designer. Like the clay pot in my example above, it doesn't say who this designer is or what His name is, but it does say very clearly and very powerfully that we (humanity) have been designed, and very intricately, for that matter. This one piece of evidence is DNA. According to ScienceDaily.com (and many other websites I found as I researched the meaning of DNA):

> Deoxyribonucleic acid (DNA) is a nucleic acid that contains the genetic instructions for the development and function of living things. All known cellular life and some viruses contain DNA. The main role of DNA in the cell is the long-term storage of information. It is often compared to a blueprint, since it contains the instructions to construct other components of the cell, such as proteins and RNA molecules. The DNA segments that carry genetic information are called genes, but other DNA sequences have structural purposes or are involved in regulating the expression of genetic information.[2]

Basically, and without getting too technical, DNA is the code, the instruction manual or the blueprint, on how to build or construct any living organism. DNA is structured code for creating a spider, a grasshopper, a dog, and even a human being. DNA proves we have design. Code, blueprints, and instruction manuals do not write themselves.

Perspective #20: DNA proves we have design. Code, blueprints, and instruction manuals do not write themselves. When you have design, you MUST have a designer!

With this level of structure, complexity, and intricacies, you must wonder, who wrote the code? Someone had to write it, create it, develop it, and design it to function the way He wanted it to, for His purpose! Remember Perspective #19: "If something has design, it MUST have a designer!" Since every living thing on this planet has DNA (evidence of

---

[2] Excerpt taken from https://www.sciencedaily.com/terms/dna.htm

a designer), we now know someone, or something exists that is greater than we are, who designed us.

Who or what this something is, I will try to explain in greater detail as we go along, but for now, we know we are created beings because we have an obvious design, and where you have design, you MUST have a designer. Where you have design, you MUST have a purpose.

From just this simple DNA example, what can we learn about this designer of ours? This designer is above us (since He designed us). The pot is never greater than the potter. This designer is far more powerful than we are, as we have been unable to design an autonomous living being out of nothing. This designer is smarter than we are. To put a copy of how to make something in every cell of that something so that every cell carries the instructions for how to make that something is pure genius!

Perspective #21: To put a copy of how to make something in every cell of that something so that every cell carries the instructions of how to make that something is pure genius!

We are not an accident. When you have a clear and deliberate design, you eliminate accidents and instead, you have purpose.

Perspective #22: We are not an accident. When you have a clear and deliberate design, you eliminate accidents and instead, you have purpose.

If this is all true, then I'm sure we can assume that He created everything else as well. For example, He placed a lot of raw materials on this planet so we could be, would be, creative just like He is. God has given us the brains, the wisdom, the passion, the desire and the problem-solving skills so we can be creative like He is.

Now that we know we have a designer, what are we going to call Him? Since He's above us, more powerful than we are and smarter than we are, let's call Him God! Since the word "God" means "the creator and ruler of the universe and source of all moral authority, the supreme being," I think the name fits. As we will find out in one of the other books in this series, He does have a name for Himself, but for now, we will refer to Him as God.

As you can see, it is not that hard to see evidence for the existence of God; all you have to do is look around. His fingerprints are everywhere. Here again, the choice is yours, to see and believe or to choose not to. Just remember Perspective #16: "God will hold you accountable for all the evidence of His existence regardless of whether you believe it or not." Just choose wisely!

To not see Him, or to refuse to see Him when it is so obvious, would be a "volitional act," not a "rational" one. This act requires a level of stubbornness that is defiant, and there is nothing I can do or say to break down a wall that refuses to budge. This kind of stubbornness may never know what God wants because they refuse to listen to Him or to acknowledge Him. You see, they think that if God doesn't exist, then they do not have to answer to Him, they are not accountable to Him. The only problem with that logic is, God doesn't require you to believe in Him for Him to exist.

Perspective #23: God doesn't need you to believe
in Him for Him to exist.

Said another way, God's existence doesn't depend on you or your belief, or better yet, God doesn't need your permission to exist.

Perspective #24: God doesn't need your permission
to exist.

You, on the other hand, are dependent on Him for the air you breathe, the food and water you consume and many other things. What does all this mean? No matter what, you must answer to Him, regardless of whether you believe in Him or not! You and only you ARE accountable to God, regardless of what you believe!

Perspective #25: You ARE accountable to God,
regardless of what you believe!

A good friend of mine, Valerie Knox, who was in a small group I was teaching at church, gave me this wonderful insight and example, which I thought was brilliant for the point I'm trying to get across here.

Valerie struggles with math but is very good at English. Her husband (Norm) is the other way around; he excels at math but struggles with English. They say that is why they make such a good team. When she was a kid in school, math would continuously frustrate her, especially the long math problems. No matter what she did, how hard she worked, how much she thought she was doing everything right, or how sincere and diligent she was. If she left out one of the variables to the math equation she was working on, she always ended up with the wrong answer. The point I want to make is, if God is NOT an integral part of your life equation, you WILL end up with the wrong answer.

Perspective #26: "If God is NOT an integral part of your life equation, you WILL end up with the wrong answer." – Valerie Knox

---

Life is extremely complicated. If you leave God out of your life equation, you will end up with the wrong answer. You are missing THE key variable to solving the equation to life.

Perspective #27: Life is extremely complicated. If you leave God out of your life equation, you will end up with the wrong answer. You are missing THE key variable to solving the equation to life.

Look at the example of so many people in this world today. They have fame, fortune, and prestige, yet they are the loneliest, sometimes most miserable people in the world. They would give anything to be happy, to be full of joy. They have been trying to solve the equation of life using Satan's key variables (sex, drugs, money, and self), and not God. Without God in your life, life for you is not what He created it to be.

Perspective #28: Without God in your life, life for
you is not what He created it to be.

If you do not believe there is a God, you are without hope. You live, you die, and then judgment. Without Him, you lose all self-value, importance, meaning and purpose for which God created you. Where is the hope in that philosophy? Where is the joy in that perspective?

There is a better way. God created you to be more than this, and deep down inside, you know this to be true. You long for this. Maybe that is why you reached out to read this book—to find out what God wants and why.

- **Perspective #13:** How much evidence will it take for you to believe God does indeed exist? To believe God does indeed love and care for you deeply?
- **Perspective #14:** Truth can be hard to find and hard to uncover.
- **Perspective #15:** Truth will always reward the diligent who sincerely seek after her and are not afraid of her.
- **Perspective #16:** God will hold you accountable for all the evidence of His existence regardless of whether you believe it or not.
- **Perspective #17:** "The finite (limited) cannot prove or disprove the existence of the infinite (unlimited)." – Skip Heitzig
- **Perspective #18:** Just because you can't see God doesn't mean He doesn't exist.
- **Perspective #19:** If something has design, it MUST have a designer.
- **Perspective #20:** DNA proves we have design. Code, blueprints, and instruction manuals do not write themselves. When you have design, you MUST have a designer!
- **Perspective #21:** To put a copy of how to make something in every cell of that something so that every cell carries the instructions of how to make that something is pure genius!
- **Perspective #22:** We are not an accident. When you have a clear and deliberate design, you eliminate accidents and instead, you have purpose.
- **Perspective #23:** God doesn't need you to believe in Him for Him to exist.
- **Perspective #24:** God doesn't need your permission to exist.
- **Perspective #25:** You ARE accountable to God, regardless of what you believe!
- **Perspective #26:** "If God is NOT an integral part of your life equation, you will end up with the wrong answer." – Valerie Knox
- **Perspective #27:** Life is extremely complicated. If you leave God out of your life equation, you will end up with the wrong answer. You are missing THE key variable to solving the equation of life.

- **Perspective #28:** Without God in your life, life for you is not what He created it to be.

Four: What Does God Want?

What does God want? This question sounds complicated. After all, God is so big and mysterious. Just the thought of answering this question might be overwhelming. Surprisingly, the answer is easier than one would think. The question is, would you like to know what God wants with you individually? What God wants of you, from you? If you knew, how would you respond to the information? Would you cooperate with God? Maybe partner with Him? Fall in love with Him and what He is doing? Does your response to the first question depend on the answer to the others?

Well, you can know what He wants, and it is quite simple. God wants a relationship! God wants a close, personal, loving, intimate relationship with you!

Perspective #29: God wants a close, personal, loving, intimate relationship with you!

This relationship with God is not just any relationship. After all, Satan has a relationship with God, although not a very good one. A true relationship with God is more than just a basic knowledge of Him; it is a close, deep friendship, a loving relationship, a partnership where you cooperate with Him and are obedient to Him and His commands. Where you honor who He is, what He says and what He wants for your life., your purpose! This relationship is close, personal and intimate, similar to a wonderful marriage relationship where you know each other so well you can finish each other's sentences.

Unfortunately, you have a problem. You see, God is perfect, righteous, holy, true and so much more, and you—not so much! Your problem is, you are a sinner, and for that matter, so am I; we all are.

For all have sinned and fall short of the glory of God. –
Romans 3:23

The *all* here in the verse above is you, me, everyone. So how can a righteous, holy God have a relationship with a sinful human being?

The truth is, He can't. Because God is righteous, holy and just, He must judge and punish ALL sin! If He does not, then He couldn't be righteous, holy, or just. He couldn't be God. Who He is demands that He judge and punish ALL sin!

This is where Jesus comes in. You see, God judged and punished Jesus for ALL of your sin, past, present, and future, even though He had not sinned. Which then allows God to accept the punishment Jesus endured on your behalf and to declare you righteous like He is. When He does this, you are now clean, free from your burden of sin, because it has been judged and punished on the cross of Jesus Christ. Which in turn, allows you to enter a close, personal, loving, intimate relationship with God because now, nothing is interfering with your relationship with God. If desired, your sin debt has been "paid in full" by Jesus Christ, which is what He wants! He remains pure and holy because He has judged and punished your sin and you get a "get out of jail free" card. Such a deal!

When you enter a relationship with God, there is only one thing you must do, and that is receive the gift of His Son Jesus Christ. There is nothing else for you to do, nothing for you to change, nothing for you to stop doing. God has already done everything needed for you to have and enter a relationship with Him. All you need to do is enter this relationship through faith in Jesus Christ, faith that Jesus paid the price you owed for the sins you've committed. The Bible is all about keeping this relationship simple.

> *For by grace you have been saved through faith. And this is not your own doing; it is the gift of God, not a result of works, so that no one may boast. For we are his workmanship, created in Christ Jesus for good works, which God prepared beforehand, that we should walk in them. – Ephesians 2:8-10*

Your relationship with God is a gift from God, but like any gift, it is a gift you must receive and open. You can't just leave it on the shelf. You see, sin interferes with and destroys your relationship with God. You may not be able to see yourself covered in sin, but God can. Since sin cannot enter His presence because He is perfect, righteous, holy, and true, He needed to judge and punish your sin before you could have a relationship with Him. Since Jesus Christ took your judgment and your punishment for you, all you need to do is receive and open the gift that He is. Jesus Christ is God's chosen way for you to enter a relationship with Him. Jesus Christ is the ONLY way for you to engage in this relationship, as God has not defined or prescribed any other way. What this means is that Jesus Christ is the bath you need to take to be cleansed of all of your sin—past, present, and future!

Perspective #30: Jesus Christ is the bath you need to take to be cleansed of all your sin—past, present, and future!

Said another way, God has prepared the bath (Jesus Christ) you need to take to cleanse you from the dirt of your sin. All you need to do is agree to take the bath!

Perspective #31: God has prepared the bath (Jesus Christ) you need to take to cleanse you from the dirt of your sin. All you need to do is agree to take the bath!

It is important for you to understand God accepts you exactly as you are and in your current condition. Then He works with you and grows you to gradually remove the things in your life that interfere with your relationship with Him. The only thing required is a belief that His Son Jesus Christ came and died for your sins. You must repent (turn away) from your sins and receive this gift of grace from Him, and finally you must desire a close, personal, loving, intimate relationship with Him as well. It IS that simple.

Sin is bondage; religious law and legalism are bondage; religion is bondage; atheism is bondage. There is only one loving relationship, and it needs to be our focus, our priority. The Bible is true and can be trusted. In it, you will find what God says about Himself, and His perspective of Himself can be trusted. Get to know Him, spend time with Him, invest time in your relationship with Him and fall more in love with Him.

Understand your enemy has a lot of tactics and strategies he uses to interfere with your relationship with God; sin is one of the biggest. Choose to invest in your relationship with Him, grow your relationship with Him, get to know Him, who He is and what He's like. When you start doing this, you can begin to live out your relationship with Him.

Back when I was throwing my 12-year temper tantrum and chose to stop talking to God, I didn't have many options. What else could I do? I was a finite being trying to punish an infinite being. I figured that with my limited power, the only thing I could do was NOT talk to Him. Unfortunately, what I didn't realize at the time was, that was one of the most painful things I could do to Him. Just ask someone who loves you dearly, "How does it feel when I do not talk to you?" You might want to add a second question, "How would you feel if I ignored you for 12 years?"

Imagine with me for a minute...

You just got married and got back from your two-week honeymoon. You had a wonderful time together, but then your spouse says or does something that ticks you off. I'm sure this has never happened to you, but what if it did? How do you think they would feel if you gave them the cold shoulder and ignored them, not for 12 years, but let's say for a week? A month?

I will almost guarantee their response will be hurt. Your spouse will be heartbroken and sad, maybe even mad, right? They may even second-guess their decision of marrying this jerk.

Now, put yourself in God's shoes. His love for you is profound and very far-reaching; it is a choice He has made. He has chosen to love you! How do you think He feels when you ignore Him? Disobey Him? Are rude, vulgar or disrespectful to Him or use His name in vain?

I can't take back the 12 years I spent mad at God, being disobedient to Him, disrespecting Him. However, I can apologize, repent and surrender again to Him. Tell Him I'm sorry and that I want what He wants—a close, personal, loving, intimate relationship.

Your next question may be, "How do we know God wants a relationship with us?"

That is another excellent question. First, that's what God had with humanity in the beginning, in the Garden of Eden. That was His purpose for creating us in His image. That is what sin destroyed. That is what Jesus' death on the cross restores. And that is what He's been trying to get back all along—a relationship with you! The purpose of this series is not only to show you WHAT God wants, but also to explain WHY He wants this and HOW you can want it as well. When we gain knowledge of Him, we also gain perspective of what He wants, they partner with each other to help us fall in love with Him.

As I'm sure you already know, any relationship requires work and effort. The more time and effort you invest in your relationships, the better those relationships are. The more time you spend getting to know the other person, the more you fall in love with them and appreciate their love for you. For example, when my wife and I got married 14 years ago, I loved her. However, I can tell you that my love for her today is far deeper, far richer than it was 14 years ago. In fact, I'm not sure I knew back then you could love someone this much. And the cool thing is, the more the two of us work on and grow our relationship with each other, and the more effort we put into it, the greater, the stronger, the deeper our love for each other gets.

How does knowing that God desires a relationship with you make you feel? You might say, "With ME? Really? Wow! Why?"

I'm sure these are just some of the responses you might have to this statement. Nevertheless, is the fact that God loves you, is pursuing you and wants a relationship with you so hard to believe? Some people may say, "Of course God wants a relationship with me; I'm so awesome." However, for most of us, when we evaluate this thought, we ask, "Why? Isn't He all-knowing? Doesn't He know who I am? What I've done? Can't He see my thoughts and how corrupt and impure they are?"

Look at me. My first perspective of God was that He was this big evil cosmic bully in Heaven who had nothing better to do than to pick on poor little (innocent) me and watch me suffer! I found out that was the furthest thing from the truth, but why was it so easy for me to believe the lie? I bought it hook, line, and sinker. I was all in. God, in my opinion at the time, was a "cosmic killjoy" ruining my life, my dreams, and punishing me with not one but TWO boys with special needs.

In reality, He was loving me and blessing me. To make me feel even worse, He continued to bless me and to love me, even when I was a jerk to Him did not understand what He was doing. I didn't even try to understand Him and what He was doing. I had pronounced judgment upon Him. He was guilty of ruining my life and since He wasn't going to talk to me and answer my questions, well then, I wasn't going to talk to Him! So there! I win. Or so I thought.

My problem, if I look back to analyze the why, was I had invested very little of the previous eight years in getting to know God, and no one was encouraging me to do so. They told me to read the Bible and they said how important it was to pray and go to church, but those things are not, in and of themselves, a relationship with God. They are tools He uses to help us get to know Him better, to learn about Him and who He is, but they are not the relationship He wants with us.

I, on the other hand, did not have the perspective that God wanted a relationship with ME! This perspective, that God wants a relationship with you, is critical if you want to get to know Him, love Him, serve Him, cooperate with Him, and partner with Him in what He's doing in His Kingdom.

Perspective #32: This perspective that God wants a relationship with you is critical if you want to get to know Him, love Him, serve Him, cooperate with Him, and partner with Him in what He's doing in His Kingdom.

It is also important if you desire to spend eternity with Him and to enjoy Him and His Kingdom forever!

By definition, a relationship is an association, connection, an affiliation, liaison, a link. However, what God wants is much deeper than that. It is a relationship that is also a friendship, a bond, an alliance, attachment, companionship, peace, goodwill, and harmony. God wants peace with you. He wants to be friends.

Perspective #33: God wants peace with you. He wants to be friends.

In addition to this, God wants you to know Him, which means God is knowable!

Perspective #34: God wants you to know Him, which means God is knowable!

This means, you can invest time in getting to know Him, if you like. Isn't it incredible to know that God, the Creator of everything, wants peace with you and He wants you to get to know Him? He wants harmony with you, and He intends to love you and be your friend. This revelation is mind-blowing when you think about it. God wants to be friends with me! Not just friends, but buddies, pals, companions, partners. Are you sure He knows what He's doing? What He's getting?

Now the question you need to ask yourself is, do YOU want a close, personal, loving, intimate relationship with HIM? This is where the rubber meets the road; what do YOU want? He's made it simple. There are no rules. You just have to receive and open the Gift of His Son Jesus Christ. You only need desire and choice to enter this relationship. The question is, do you want one with Him?

Some of you may say, "Well, let me clean myself up and make myself presentable first." Hogwash! He doesn't require this, so why should you? He is willing to accept you exactly the way you are today, right now, this minute, this second, sin and all. He will take care of "cleaning you up" later. Of course, this will take time, but that is not the point. If you want a relationship with Him, then by default, you also want Him to clean your life up.

You need to understand the dynamics of what is going on. You see, we (humans) are at war with God. In the Garden of Eden, we rebelled against God and His commands for our lives. We chose to "do our own thing" and to work in close cooperation with God's enemy to try to destroy Him and His plans for humanity. To have a relationship with Him, we must first change sides. To have a relationship with God, you must first surrender your life to Him.

Perspective #35: To have a relationship with God, you must first surrender your life to Him.

This means that God's conditions for a relationship with Him are surrender—complete, absolute, and total surrender!

Perspective #36: God's conditions for a relationship with Him are surrender—complete, absolute, and total surrender!

Surrender means you humble yourself and say, "God, I was wrong, you are right. I repent of my sins. I turn from my sins and towards You God; forgive me! By faith, I believe your Son Jesus Christ died for my sins and I accept and open your gift of grace to me. Help me to possess this gift, help me to desire a relationship with You, help me to invest in my relationship with You, help me to fall in love with You. Show me how!"[3]

Are you willing to invest in your relationship with Him? Are you willing to make your relationship with Him the most important relationship in your life? Are you willing to value your relationship with Him as much as He does? Are you willing to invest in your relationship as much as He has?

I bet you thought I was going to be easy on you? Well, as George H.W. Bush and Dana Carvey used to say, "Not going to do it, wouldn't be prudent!"

I know these are strong commitments, but He wants to be that kind of friend with you. One where you do everything together, you are committed to each other, and you would give your life for each other. The depth of this relationship with God is so hard to put into words, but just a small portion of it outstrips the depth and love of any other relationship you have ever had or experienced. The greatness is off the charts!

Some people already know they want a relationship with God; it is an easy decision for them. Others may say they already have a relationship with God through their church, religion, mosque, synagogue, temple, meditation, etc. They explain, "I'm spiritual, just not

---

[3] See Appendix A for a simple prayer that will lead you through this process.

religious." Let me clarify, God does not want a relationship with you through a third party. He wants a relationship with YOU personally!

Perspective #37: God does not want a relationship with you through a third party. He wants a relationship with YOU personally!

Understand, this is not a drive-by relationship where you put in a little face time on Sunday and say, "I'm good for the rest of the week." It is not a spiritual" relationship either, where you think about Him on occasion and pretty much do your own thing and let Him do His thing. How are you going to get to know Him, especially when there is so much of Him to know, when you invest very little time and effort in doing so?

Let me give you an example of what I'm talking about. In the book of Matthew, towards the end of the Sermon on the Mount, Jesus says some profound things:

Not everyone who says to me, "Lord, Lord," will enter the kingdom of heaven, but the one who does the will of my Father who is in heaven. On that day many will say to me, "Lord, Lord, did we not prophesy in your name, and cast out demons in your name, and do many mighty works in your name?" And then will I declare to them, "I never knew you; depart from me, you workers of lawlessness." – Matthew 7:21-23

Why would Jesus say "depart from me, you workers of lawlessness" to people who appear to have done great things for Him and His Kingdom? There is only one reason: He doesn't know them because they never invested time in a relationship with Him personally. Oh sure, they may have had a connection with some other earthly distraction (church, religion, mosque, synagogue, temple, meditation, spirituality, etc.), but not with Him and His Father.

In their book *I Don't Have Enough Faith to be an Atheist*, Norm Geisler and Frank Turek give an incredible example of this when they say (and I'm paraphrasing here):

Imagine one evening; you are sitting at home, working on a puzzle or playing a board-game with your family and you hear a knock at the door. You go to the front door, and you see a stranger. You open the door and ask, "How can I help you?" They proceed to try to come into your house as if they know you as if you are good friends. You say, "Hold on a minute, I do not know you. Get out of my house, get off my property!" (Or something like that.)

Later that evening, you are still having a good time with your family, and you hear another knock at the door. You once again go to the front door, and you see your parents there who have come over to visit you and their grandbabies! How do you respond to them? You hug them, ask how they are doing, how they have been? Why the different responses? Quite frankly, you know them. You have a "relationship" with them. The other person you didn't have a clue who they were, but mom and dad you have known well for the past however many years of your life.

Why would God be any different? Why would God let you into His house (Heaven) if you have spent little time or effort in getting to know Him? If you, being a flawed, sinful human being wouldn't do this, what makes you think a perfect, holy, righteous being would?

Understand, there are three levels of "knowing." You can "know of" someone. For example, I know of Billy Graham. I've seen him preach on TV, but I do not know him personally. I've never had a face-to-face conversation with him. If I went over to his house to spend the night, he'd probably send me packing.

Next, you can "know about" someone. For example, I've read some of Billy Graham's books where he talks about his family, especially the love of his life, Ruth. I may know a little bit more "about" Billy Graham. However, I still do not "know" him personally. I do not know what kind of ice cream he likes or even if he likes ice cream.

The only way to get to "know" someone is to invest the time it takes to do so. To "know" God requires an investment in the time it takes to get to know Him.

Perspective #38: To "know" God requires an investment in the time it takes to get to know Him.

Because He is "all-knowing," God may know of you. He may even know about you. However, since you have invested very little time in getting to know Him, He doesn't know you personally. You never took the time to share your life with Him, involving Him in it. God is NEVER an intruder in our lives – He is only an invited guest.

Perspective #39: "God is NEVER an intruder in our lives – He is only an invited guest." – Michael Franzese

---

Maybe you are like I was, blaming God for everything that goes wrong in your life rather than investing the time to get to know Him and seeing how much He loves you. As human beings, we have this horrible habit of judging God based on what we "think" He's doing, not who we know Him to be. I was a professional God-blamer; I know all about this. Do you think this would be the case if you just invested some time to get to know Him personally?

Another question you need to ask yourself is, why would you want to spend eternity (forever and ever and ever) worshipping someone you spend very little time getting to know? Wouldn't this just irk you to no end? Having to "worship" someone you do not care for?

Without a relationship, there is NO WAY for you get to know Him! You may have a façade of a relationship with Him, but you have never really invested any time in getting to know Him personally. You are only interested in what you can get out of Him. You are looking to impress other people or to satisfy a spouse. Maybe you are just looking for fire insurance or how He is going to help you get what you want. Hoping that He's going to grade you on a curve, that your "good deeds" outweigh your "bad deeds," and because of that, He HAS to let you in.

Let me give you this example I heard in church recently from my pastor. Let's say you are 51% good and 49% bad. That is, you are "mostly" good. Your good deeds out-weigh your bad deeds. You think you've been good enough, so God should just accept you. I know this sounds good. However, let's apply this logic to an apple pie. Would you eat an apple pie that had 51% good apple pie ingredients and 49% horse manure?[4] If you wouldn't do this, then why would you expect God to do this?

God will not let "dirty people" into His clean Kingdom. He cleans everyone who enters. Or more accurately, He cleans everyone who chooses to be cleaned. If you are relying on God to let you into heaven since your good deeds outweigh your bad deeds, then you are in danger of hearing Jesus say to you, "I never knew you." God forbid!

Jesus mentions that "only the one who does the will of my Father" will enter His Kingdom. What do you think the "will" of the Father is?

And one of the scribes came up and heard them disputing with one another, and seeing that he answered them well, asked him, "Which commandment is the most important of all?" Jesus answered, "The most important is, 'Hear, O Israel: The Lord our God, the Lord is one[5]. And you shall love the Lord your God with all your heart and with all your soul and with all your mind and with all your strength. [6]' The second is this: 'You shall love your neighbor as yourself.'[7] There is no other commandment greater than these." – Mark 12:28-31

Notice that both commands are relational—relational to God and then relational to others. This relational picture forms the shape of a cross: first upwards to God then outwards to others.

---

[4] Paraphrased from a message by Pastor Ron Woods, The Well Church, Yucaipa, CA.
[5] Or the Lord our God is one Lord.
[6] Deut. 6:4-5 - Hear, O Israel: The Lord our God, the Lord is one. You shall love the Lord your God with all your heart and with all your soul and with all your might.
[7] Lev. 19:18 - You shall not take vengeance or bear a grudge against the sons of your own people, but you shall love your neighbor as yourself: I am the Lord.

The first and most important relationship God wants you to have is with Him, through His Son Jesus, empowered by the Holy Spirit. He wants you to invest in that relationship. If you do not have this, then you're missing what's essential. Also, if you do not have a close, personal, loving, intimate relationship with God, you can't have a very good relationship with others. You will not be empowered to complete His second command for you.

Now, before you jump in and say this sounds like "works," it is work in the same way that all relationships are work. They do not come easy. You can't sit back and do nothing and still have a relationship. Relationships require action on both sides to be relationships. It is not working to "earn" your salvation. That "work" was all done by God, Jesus, and the Holy Spirit on the cross. However, it is the work of investing in your relationship with God and spending the time it takes to get to know all about Him!

Understand that a relationship with God means you desire to get to know Him and who He is. You want to honor Him in everything you do, say and think.

Perspective #40: Understand that a relationship with God means you desire to get to know Him and who He is. You want to honor Him in everything you do, say and think.

You want to be obedient to Him and His commands, even if you do not agree with them. A relationship with God is choosing to fall in love with Him. It is choosing to be grateful for Him and for what He's done for you.

Perspective #41: A relationship with God is choosing to fall in love with Him. It is choosing to be grateful for Him and for what He's done for you.

Let's face it, a relationship is work. Your relationship with God will not be any different. It will require you to work at it, require you to want it, require you to invest in it, require you to get to know Him personally. The more you know Him, the better you can understand Him and what He does or allows to happen in your life. He may even test you to see if you want this relationship with Him by giving you two very precious boys with special needs. He may do this to see if you will trust Him, even when you can't see or know what is going on.

This "work" is no different than your relationship with your spouse, your family, your friends, or your co-workers. Every relationship requires work on both parts to be a valid relationship. There is no such thing as a one-sided relationship; both sides must work at it. If they do not, then it ceases to be a relationship. However, your relationship with God is at an entirely different level than any other relationship in your life. First, you need to understand you have the EXACT relationship with God YOU want!

Perspective #42: You have the EXACT relationship
with God YOU want!

What this means is you are the one controlling your relationship with God. Your level of intimacy with God, your level of friendship with God, your level of partnership and cooperation with God, and your level of love for God are all under your power and control!

Perspective #43: Your level of intimacy with God,
your level of friendship with God, your level of
partnership and cooperation with God, and your level
of love for God are all under your power and control!

To make things more difficult, to make the "work" seem harder, you have an enemy who hates you almost as much as he hates God. This enemy will do everything he can to interfere and distract you from your relationship with God. I think he does this because he can't affect God directly, so he will do everything he can to hurt God indirectly through you. This requires you to be focused, to be diligent and for you to persevere through challenges, trials, and difficulties that may come your way, even when you do not understand the WHY. The only way for you to do this is to invest the time it takes to know the One who loves you so much, who gave everything to redeem you, to make way for you to enter into this relationship with Him.

You see, God has already done His part to prove to you He loves you and desires a relationship with you by taking care of your biggest problem: sin. You need to do your part by first believing Jesus died for your sins and then by faith, putting that belief into action by desiring a relationship with God as well, and then investing in that relationship with Him. Invest in getting to know Him personally.

Understanding this, my next question for you is, if you can have as much of God as you want, how much of God will you take?

Perspective #44: If you can have as much of God as you want, how much of God will you take?

What if I were to put one trillion dollars (that is 999,999,999,999 dollars + one dollar) in front of you and said, "You can have as much of this money as you want," how much would you take? Would you take $5 million? After all, you do not want to be greedy. With $5 million, you could retire with an income of $250,000 a year for 20 years. That is almost five times the average annual U.S. household income of $55,775, which means you could retire for 20 years with nearly five times the average U.S. income. Maybe $5 million is not enough? Maybe you would take $5 billion. That should keep you happy for a couple of years, right?

Why not take all of it? Why not take one trillion dollars? Why not want ALL of it?

Your relationship with God is like the example above. However, God is far more valuable, far more precious. Therefore, why not take ALL of Him you can handle? Why not desire ALL of Him you can have? Why not invest all you can in your relationship with Him? I guarantee it will take you ALL of eternity just to get to know and love and appreciate all of who He is. He is one investment you won't be sorry you made!

In Matthew Chapter 13, Jesus tells a couple of parables that illustrate this fact:

---

*The kingdom of heaven is like treasure hidden in a field, which a man found and covered up. Then in his joy he goes and **sells all that he has** and buys that field. Again, the kingdom of heaven is like a merchant in search of fine* *pearls, who, on finding one pearl of great value, went and* **sold all that he had** *and bought it. – Matthew 13:44-46, emphasis added*

Jesus wants us to be just like this man and this merchant. When we recognize the treasure that is in Him, we run off and sell everything we have and invest it in Him and in His Kingdom.

That means we own nothing else but Him; we've sold EVERYTHING to possess Him. There is nothing we own that is hindering our relationship with Him. We are free of all encumbrances!

Notice how Jesus wants us to get rid of all the other distractions, all the other things in our lives that interfere with our relationship with Him!

Perspective #45: Jesus wants us to get rid of all the other distractions, all the other things in our lives that interfere with our relationship with Him!

Now, He may or may not ask you to sell all your possessions to follow Him. However, He will put His finger on the ones He feels interfere with your relationship with Him, which is what we want Him to do. We want Him to remove anything and everything from our lives that interfere with us getting to know Him better and investing entirely in our relationship with Him. And this is what it means to be in a relationship with God.

Your ability to have the correct perspective depends on you being able to humble yourself before God and say, "I am sorry, I repent, I surrender. God, I want a relationship with You."

If you do want to develop a close, personal, relationship with God the Father, the Creator of the universe, that is an awesome thing! However, if this is something you think you cannot do, let me ask you to make a promise to yourself right now. Make a pledge that says, "I will keep an open mind as I read through this series and see if what this Walker guy says makes sense." If it does, then you can choose for yourself later whether you want this relationship with God or not.

- **Perspective #29:** God wants a close, personal, loving, intimate relationship with you!
- **Perspective #30:** Jesus Christ is the bath you need to take to be cleansed of all your sin-past, present, and future!
- **Perspective #31:** God has prepared the bath (Jesus Christ) you need to take to cleanse you from the dirt of your sin. All you need to do is agree to take the bath!
- **Perspective #32:** This perspective that God wants a relationship with you is critical if you want to get to know Him, love Him, serve Him, cooperate with Him, partner with Him in what He's doing in His Kingdom.
- **Perspective #33:** God wants peace with you. He wants to be friends.
- **Perspective #34:** God wants you to know Him, which means God is knowable!
- **Perspective #35:** To have a relationship with God, you must first surrender your life to Him.
- **Perspective #36:** God's conditions for a relationship with Him are surrender—complete, absolute, and total surrender!
- **Perspective #37:** God does not want a relationship with you through a third party. He wants a relationship with YOU personally!
- **Perspective #38:** To "know" God requires an investment in the time it takes to get to know Him.
- **Perspective #39:** "God is NEVER an intruder in our lives – He is only an invited guest." – Michael Franzese
- **Perspective #40:** Understand that a relationship with God means you desire to get to know Him and who He is. You want to honor Him in everything you do, say and think.
- **Perspective #41:** A relationship with God is choosing to fall in love with Him. It is choosing to be grateful for Him and what He's doing for you!
- **Perspective #42:** You have the EXACT relationship with God YOU want!
- **Perspective #43:** Your level of intimacy with God, your level of friendship with God, your level of partnership and cooperation

with God, and your level of love for God are all under your power and control!

- **Perspective #44:** If you can have as much of God as you want, how much of God will you take?
- **Perspective #45:** Jesus wants us to get rid of all the other distractions, all the other things in our lives that interfere with our relationship with Him!

Five: Questions

Is God afraid of your questions? God is NEVER afraid of your questions!

Perspective #46: God is NEVER afraid of your questions!

Is there anything a finite being (you) could ask an infinite being (God) that would stump Him? That would confuse Him or cause Him to say, "Hmmm, well, I never thought of it that way." Probably not, and that is why God LOVES it when you ask questions!

The reason God is never afraid of your questions is because they show Him that you are trying to understand, trying to learn and trying to grow. As soon as you start asking questions, He gets excited because you start doing precisely what He designed you to do: learn and grow, comprehend and understand, discern and decipher Him and all that He's created for you to discover!

The problem He has is when you let the fact that you have questions or doubts discourage you from pursuing a relationship with Him. Allowing those questions and doubts to interfere with you taking the time to invest in and grow your relationship with Him.

God will always know the truth that is in your heart. You cannot deceive Him. He knows all things. You can only fool yourself and others. When you allow questions and doubts to turn into unbelief or refusal to believe, you fail to reach the full potential for which God created you. You are not the successful person God wants you to become. When you allow questions or doubts to keep you from investing in your relationship with God, you quit, you give up, which means you have failed. The only difference between success and failure is "success" NEVER gives up!

Perspective #47: The only difference between success and failure is "success" NEVER gives up!

There is a fine line that separates those who are successful in this world from those who are failures. This line of separation is perseverance. Successful people never give up.

Perspective #48: There is a fine line that separates those who are successful in this world from those who are failures. This line of separation is perseverance. Successful people never give up.

This doesn't mean successful people never fail. Failing is learning. Successful people learn more from failure than they do from success, just ask them. One of the most important things they learn is to never give up.

That is what God wants you to do. Never give up on your relationship with Him. Never let questions or doubts interfere with your relationship with Him. Accept the fact that you are a finite being not capable of knowing everything and of having all the answers. Once you do this, you can say, "Well, I'm not too sure about that," or "I do not know the answer to that question, but I do know that God loves me and wants a close, personal relationship with me!"

Understand, this isn't settling. It doesn't mean an answer to your question doesn't exist; it just means you do not have the answer right now or you may not be ready for the answer. Let me give you an example. In Genesis we read:

And God said, "Let there be light," and there was light. And God saw that the light was good. And God separated the light from the darkness. God called the light Day, and the darkness he called Night. And there was evening and there was morning, the first day. – Genesis 1:3-5)

A few verses later we read:

And God said, "Let there be lights in the expanse of the heavens to separate the day from the night. And let them be for signs and for seasons, and for days and years, and let them be lights in the expanse of the heavens to give light upon the earth." And it was so. And God made the

---

two great lights—the greater light to rule the day and the lesser light to rule the night—and the stars. And God set them in the expanse of the heavens to give light on the earth, to rule over the day and over the night, and to separate the light from the darkness. And God saw that it was good. And there was evening and there was morning, the fourth day. – Genesis 1:14-19

The question this might raise in your mind is if there are day and evening on the first day, but the sun and moon aren't created until the fourth day, so how can you have a day and evening without the sun and the moon?

What a great question. The difficulty in grasping how this could be will usually come from an incorrect perspective of God and of this universe He's created. First off, you do not need the sun or the oon to have day and evening; all you need is the rotation of the earth and light. The earth rotates on its axis once every 24 hours, or what we call one day. Now, to have day and evening, the only other thing you need besides rotation is light. In 1 John we read:

This is the message we have heard from him and proclaim to you, that God is light, and in him is no darkness at all. – 1 John 1:5

Now you know the source of the light. Once you understand these subtle nuances, you can easily see how you can have day and evening without the sun and moon because God is the light shining on the earth. Mystery solved.

You may not agree with this answer, that, of course, is something God has given you the freedom to do. Whether you agree or not, is not the point, that has more to do with your volition rather than truth, questions or doubt. God has purposefully not answered all our questions. As we invest time in getting to know Him, we begin to see how He uses our questions to grow and strengthen our relationship with Him. It's clever when you think about it. He designed us to be curious, to be inquisitive, to draw us closer to Himself.

Questions are not meant to discourage you; they are meant to encourage you to seek and find an answer. When you have questions, it doesn't mean you give up and quit seeking the answer; it means you pray and ask God to reveal the answer to you. It could be that you are not ready for the answer just yet. Maybe you need to learn a few more things about God before you can comprehend the one thing you are questioning. Be patient and understand that God is knowable, and God WANTS you to know Him. If He wants you to know Him, then He wants you to have the answers to your questions.

The key thing we need to learn is to ask the right questions. Or, better yet, ask the questions in the right way. With God, WHY is rarely the right question. It is a "defensive" question; it says, "God, you best be explaining yourself to me" which is not conducive to the close, personal, loving, intimate relationship God wants. Asking God why just shows our ignorance of who He is. God, being God, does not have to defend Himself to you. He doesn't owe you an answer to a "why" question. For that matter, God doesn't owe anyone an answer to a "why" question!

Perspective #49: God doesn't owe anyone an
answer to a "why" question!

Put yourself in God's shoes. Would you want to answer billions upon billions of "why" questions 24 hours a day, seven days a week? Most of them over and over again? If this is something you wouldn't do, then why would you expect God too? Instead, He's empowered His creation with problem-solving skills. True, we don't always use them correctly; however, if our passion, if our desire is for a relationship with Him as well, then and only then are we capable of cooperating with Him to see the truth, know the truth and embrace His truth!

Besides, He is the Creator of ALL things, and as the Creator, He doesn't owe His creation an answer. I know this doesn't usually sit well with us and our arrogance; however, that doesn't mean it is any less true. Does the potter owe the pot an explanation of why he made the pot the way he did? No, he does not. The potter is free to make the pot any way he chooses and for whatever purpose he chooses. The pot needs to get over itself and accept how it was made.

God does not feel it necessary always to be defending Himself and His decisions. Therefore, the "why" question is often a bad one to ask God. There is a better way. Instead of asking God, "why" ask Him "what" and "how." For example, "What does this mean?" or "How can you?" If we apply this to our earlier question, we get "What does this mean that you start marking time (day and evening) before you create the sun and the moon?" or "How can you have day and evening without the sun and moon?" I always like to add, "Lord, help me to understand this magnificent creation of yours better!"

When we do this, we change our attitude and our perspective from demanding answers of God, to one of cooperating with God, even though we don't understand what He is doing or why.

Another thing we need to know and understand is that questions challenge and validate our thinking, allowing us to go through the process of justifying what we believe and why.

Perspective #50: Questions challenge and validate our thinking, allowing us to go through the process of justifying what we believe and why.

We should never be afraid of questions. We should be excited for them, as they allow us to leverage and grow our minds to know more about Him. When we know more about Him, we can fall more in love with Him. Because we fall more in love with Him, we want to know more about Him. It's a beautiful cycle of wonder and growth that can only be found in Him.

Questions can come to us from two different directions: questions we have about God (internal) and questions other people ask us about God (external).

At one time, I was scared to death of external questions. I would be paralyzed with fear whenever someone had a question for me about why I believe what I believe. Most likely, because I believed without knowing the answer or committing the answer to memory. I believed what I believed, but I wasn't comfortable explaining the answers to the tough questions others would bring to me.

Let me give you an example. One day, several years ago at work, a group of us were talking about God during one of our breaks. A very good female friend of mine said something like, "How do you know God is not a woman?" Good question, right? You would think, for someone who has been learning about God for years, this is a pretty easy one to answer. However, I froze in fear because, at the time, I wasn't prepared to respond correctly and with love. Now, I know this is embarrassing, but I need to make the point.

After spending a couple of hours with God telling Him how embarrassed, sorry and ashamed I was because I couldn't defend Him and didn't have an answer, He lovingly helped me to realize that I did know the answer, I just wasn't prepared to present it. My perspective needed adjusting. Instead of thinking that everyone will see God as I see Him and say, "That is so obvious," I needed to anticipate that people have questions about God—good, valid, legitimate questions that need answers.

Understand, the answers to most questions are there, you just may or may not like the answer. Nonetheless, just because you do not like an answer, doesn't mean you shouldn't invest some time into getting to know God better. The more you know about who God is, the better you will be able to understand the answer.

Back to the question of how do we know God is not a woman. Jesus always called God "Father," He never called God "Mother." Also, Jesus was born of a virgin woman, meaning He had a mother and God was His Father. Therefore, God is masculine or male; God is NOT a woman (sorry ladies). Obviously, my fear of the question was unfounded.

Lesson learned. If for some reason you do not know the answer to a question someone asks you about God, look at this as an opportunity and say, "That is a GREAT question. Let me research and get back to you with the answer. Are there any other questions about God that I can answer or find out the answer for you as well?"

What this does is give you three opportunities. One, you get to find out the answer for yourself and grow in your faith, knowledge, and understanding of your relationship with God. Two, you get to continue your conversation about God with someone who is curious. And three, you get to relish the joy of sharing God and His love with someone else.

What a blessing and an opportunity that is! Be grateful for them, cherish them, thank God for them and their questions, and always ask God for the wisdom to represent Him to others properly. After all, once we enter a relationship with Him, His desire is for us to go on and to represent Him well to others.

One of the most important skills you can develop in answering "external" questions is listening. Listen to the person who is asking the question. Listen to the question. Repeat it back to make sure you understand it correctly as well. And whatever you do, don't jump into a "bible-badgering" session with them. They may not know God the way you do, for that matter, they may not know the Bible the way you do. Go easy on them, don't be James and John reigning down fire and brimstone on them because they don't get it, or they don't understand. God has given you a command, love others. He didn't tell you to destroy others with your biblical knowledge and prowess, be love to them, help them to fall in love with God. You have an amazing opportunity in front of you; don't waste it by judging, enjoy it by sharing Him and His love!

The point I'm trying to make here is that you should avoid "debating" or "arguing" with others about God, as this is a combative position. Debates and arguments take a "right vs. wrong" approach. It is far more loving, productive and kind if you "discuss" Him and His Kingdom with others. This requires communication, and for communication to exist, you must first "listen" to what the other person is saying. When you listen before you attempt to communicate His truth, you are doing a much better job at reflecting Him and His love to other people.

Way too often, Christians take a "know it all" approach and try to bludgeon people with the truth and the Gospel. How is this loving? How is this kind? Especially when you do not take the time to listen to what they have to say, you interrupt them and tell them how it "really" is. Now you may be right in your theology, but you are so very wrong in your approach. Notice what Paul says to the Corinthians:

> *Be watchful, stand firm in the faith, act like men, be strong.* **_Let all that you do be done in love_**. *– 1 Corinthians 16:13-14, emphasis added*

The "let all that you do be done in love" exhortation is the hard part. Since Jesus is our example, spend some time and study His life, His ministry and His interactions with people. Jesus rarely got mad, angry or frustrated with people. He did everything in love, with a loving heart, truly caring about and for the soul of the person He was interacting with. We should do the same. People didn't always like how Jesus answered their questions. Why would we expect anything different? For example, look at the rich man that asked Jesus what he must do to inherit eternal life:

> *And a ruler asked him, "Good Teacher, what must I do to inherit eternal life?" And Jesus said to him, "Why do you call me good? No one is good except God alone. You know the commandments: 'Do not commit adultery, Do not murder, Do not steal, Do not bear false witness, Honor your father and mother.'*[8]*" And he said, "All these I have kept from my youth." When Jesus heard this, he said to him, "One thing you still lack. Sell all that you have and distribute to the poor, and you will have treasure in heaven; and come, follow me." But when he heard these things, he became very sad, for he was extremely rich. – Luke 18:18-23*

The rich man was sincere in his question; he truly wanted to know what he must do to inherit eternal life. Maybe he thought the answer would be easy, after all, he had great wealth, and he could "buy" his way through anything. However, he doesn't like the answer Jesus gives him.

Jesus always had a way of putting His finger right on what the problem was with people. In the case of the rich man in the story above, his wealth was interfering with his relationship with God. He wanted

---

[8] See the 10 Commandments in either Exodus 20:12-16 or Deuteronomy 5:16-20.

eternal life, but he didn't want to give up everything for it. Notice how painful Jesus' answer is to the rich man. He (the rich man) became very sad after he had heard what Jesus said to him. Why? Because he was very wealthy, his world revolved around material things; he may not have known how he could exist apart from them. And now this Jewish teacher is telling him to get rid of it all and give it to the poor. We do not know if the man ever did what Jesus told him to do; unlike Paul Harvey, the Bible doesn't always tell us "the rest of the story." However, God wants complete obedience and loyalty from us. After all, He purchased us with the blood of His Son, He owns us and wants nothing to come in between us and our relationship with Him. Even though it may be difficult to do, we must always remove any obstacle to our relationship with God.

Perspective #51: Even though it may be difficult to do, we must always remove any obstacle to our relationship with God.

Finally, people will often use the phrase "I think" or "I feel" when it comes to God. That may be all well and good, but it is irrelevant. As I said earlier, what we feel or what we think does not matter. In the end, the only thing that matters is what God feels and thinks, and that my friend is what we should be basing our relationship with Him on. What God feels, what God thinks, what God wants should be our only foundation!

Do not be afraid of questions. They are good and will help you grow in your relationship with God. As you go through this series, keep a notepad handy so you can jot down your questions and either research them or ask them online at WalkerJamesAuthor.com.

Perspective Recap:

- **Perspective #46:** God is NEVER afraid of your questions!
- **Perspective #47:** The only difference between success and failure is "success" NEVER gives up!
- **Perspective #48:** There is a fine line that separates those who are successful in this world from those who are failures. This line of separation is perseverance. Successful people never give up.
- **Perspective #49:** God doesn't owe anyone an answer to a "why" question!
- **Perspective #50:** Questions challenge and validate our thinking, allowing us to go through the process of justifying what we believe and why.
- **Perspective #51:** Even though it may be difficult to do, we must always remove any obstacle to our relationship with God.

Six: Be Sincere

Most questions come in two flavors: "sincere," where you are truly seeking to know and understand His truth, and "insincere," where you do not care about Him or a relationship with Him. You want to make fun of Him or His children, or you are just lazy and want to justify your lack of belief in His existence.

You can find sincere questions throughout the Bible. For example, in the Book of Matthew, Chapter 18, Peter asks Jesus a question:

Then Peter came up and said to him, "Lord, how often will my brother sin against me, and I forgive him? As many as seven times?" – Matthew 18:21

Jesus kindly answered Peter's question by saying:

Jesus said to him, "I do not say to you seven times, but seventy-seven times.[9] – Matthew 18:22

Notice Jesus' answer sets the bar high for how often we are to forgive our brother or sister who sins against us. He goes on to illustrate why this is the case by telling Peter the story of the king and the unforgiving servant. In this story, the king is God who has forgiven you (the servant) of an enormous debt (all your sin). Think about it: If you do not forgive others of the small debt, in comparison to the debt God has forgiven you, then why should God forgive you? How can God forgive you?

If Peter didn't ask this question of Jesus, we might not have such an amazing answer to help us in our walk and relationship with Him and with others.

Answers to most of the questions we have can be found in the Bible when someone else has asked the same question. That is why reading the Bible needs to become an integral part of our relationship

---

[9] Some translations have seventy times seven. Whether seventy times seven or seventy-seven times, both imply you are always to forgive your brother or sister who sins against you.

with God. It answers a lot of questions we may have about our relationship with Him. It may, hopefully, even create some additional questions as well. Do not let this scare you. As I said, questions are a good thing. Just make sure you are seeking answers from a reputable source, someone who believes the Bible is the inerrant, infallible, authoritative Word of God. If they do not believe this, then their God is microscopic. You might not want to trust anything they say because, in their minds and hearts, God is limited in what He can and can't do.

Sometimes answers require background knowledge and understanding. A good example of this would be a section of Proverbs I was reading recently. I started reading one chapter of Proverbs each day several years ago based on the recommendation of Pastor Skip Heitzig, whose messages I listen to all the time. Proverbs is an easy one to do this with because it has 31 chapters in it, one for every day of the month. If a month doesn't have 31 days in it, I will read through Chapter 31 on the last day of the month so I'm back to chapter one on the first of the month.

I was reading through Proverbs chapter 26 when I came across this section:

Answer not a fool according to his folly, lest you be like him yourself. Answer a fool according to his folly, lest he be wise in his own eyes. – Proverbs 26:4-5

I'd been reading this every month for over a year, and every time I came to it, it bugged me. Do not answer a fool? Do answer a fool? What am I supposed to do? I would pray and ask God for the wisdom, but for some reason, I wasn't getting it. Finally, I took my own advice and searched the Internet to see what others were saying about it, and I found an answer on the website GotQuestions.org.[10] Since I had been to the site several times over the course of writing this book, I had come to trust and respect their opinion greatly. I was immediately drawn to see what they had to say.

---

[10] See http://www.gotquestions.org/Proverbs-26-4-5.html

The question they were answering was: "Do Proverbs 26:4 and 26:5 contradict each other? How can both verses be true?" which was precisely the question I had. Here's what they said:

Proverbs has much to say about fools. They despise wisdom (Proverbs 1:7, 22, 10:21, 23:9); they are right in their own eyes (Proverbs 12:15); they are deceitful (Proverbs 14:8) and scornful (Proverbs 10:23, 14:9). The wise are also given instruction on how to deal with fools in Proverbs. Instructing a fool is pointless because his speech is full of foolishness (Proverbs 15:2, 14) and he does not want wisdom and understanding (Proverbs 18:2).

The futility of trying to impart wisdom to a fool is the basis of Proverbs 26:4-5, which tell us how to answer a fool. These seemingly contradictory verses are actually a common form of parallelism found in the Old Testament, where one idea builds upon another. Verse 4 warns against arguing with a fool on his own terms, lest we stoop to his level and become as foolish as he is. Because he despises wisdom and correction, the fool will not listen to wise reason and will try to draw us into his type of argument, whether it is by using deceit, scoffing at our wisdom, or becoming angry and abusive. If we allow him to draw us into this type of discourse, we are answering him "according to his folly" in the sense of becoming like him.

The phrase "according to his folly" in verse 5, on the other hand, tells us that there are times when a fool has to be addressed so that his foolishness will not go unchallenged. In this sense answering him according to his folly means to expose the foolishness of his words, rebuking him on the basis of his folly so he will see the idiocy of his words and reasoning. Our "answer" in this case is to be one of reproof, showing him the truth so he might see the foolishness of his words in the light of reason. Even though he will most likely despise and reject the wisdom offered to him, we are to make the attempt, both for the sake of the truth which is always to be declared and for the sake of those listening, that they may see the difference between wisdom and folly and be instructed.

Whether we use the principle of verse 4 and deal with a fool by ignoring him, or obey verse 5 and reprove a fool depends on the situation. In matters of insignificance, it's probably better to disregard him. In more important areas, such as when a fool denies the existence of God (Psalm 14:1), verse 5 tells us to respond to his foolishness with words of rebuke and instruction. To let a fool speak his nonsense without reproof encourages him to remain wise in his own eyes and possibly gives credibility to his folly in the eyes of others.

As you can see, what appeared somewhat confusing is quite logical and makes a lot of sense once explained. If you have ever dealt with foolish people, you know they do not care about truth and wisdom; you can appreciate the insight in these two approaches.

A good friend of mine shared this quote his mother always said. "Never argue with a fool in public. Nobody knows who the fool is!"

Perspective #52: "Never argue with a fool in public. Nobody knows who the fool is!" – Maureen Rose Plein

---

Some great wisdom. I also found a similar quote attributed to Mark Twain that I thought was equally as poignant. "Never argue with a fool in public. They will drag you down to their level and then beat you with experience!"

Perspective #53: "Never argue with a fool in public. They will drag you down to their level and then beat you with experience." – Mark Twain

---

I think the point both perspectives are making is, choose your battles wisely. Also, always be sure to validate the answers others give you. There are a lot of wolves in sheep's clothing out there (a.k.a. fools) whose sole purpose is to confuse, distract, dissuade or to create doubt in God's children. Use the power of the Holy Spirit to help you in discerning the truth of God. Understand that God will not hold you accountable for what someone else says about Him; He will only hold you accountable for what you believe is true!

Perspective #54: God will not hold you accountable for what someone else says about Him; He will only hold you accountable for what you believe is true.

So, be careful, do your research and search the Scriptures. Take the time to know and understand what you believe and why. Notice, that is exactly what the Berean followers did.

The brothers immediately sent Paul and Silas away by night to Berea, and when they arrived they went into the Jewish synagogue. Now these Jews were more noble than those in Thessalonica; they received the word with all eagerness, examining the Scriptures daily to see if these things were so. – Acts 17:10-11

Ask God; He is not afraid of your questions. God wants you to sincerely want to know more about Him, which means, He is knowable. Pursue Him and get to know Him. Leverage your questions to grow and strengthen your relationship with Him. God is excited to teach you, to grow you and to guide you. His passion and His desire is to help you fall more in love with Him and with who He is!

Perspective #55: God is excited to teach you, to grow you and to guide you! His passion and His desire is to help you fall more in love with Him and with who He is!

You may also find several questions have several possible answers to them. Here, you need to ask God to help you, by the power of

His Holy Spirit, to discern which answer is correct or which answer is most correct. Understand that sometimes several answers may be correct and none of the answers may be correct. A lot of times, it may depend on how the question is worded. Be sensitive to how a question is stated or phrased as the question may be designed to cause you to question your relationship with God. These types of questions are purposefully destructive, and the only way to combat them is to compare the question to what you DO know about God, not what you don't know. We will talk more about how to do this in some of the other books of this series. For now, just be sensitive to the fact that not all questions are sincere.

Sometimes, it may even feel like God is not or does not want to answer your questions. You pray and ask, but it feels like your prayers are bouncing off a brick wall. For example, you may be going through a struggle, and you may have reached out to God many times over the last several days, but it feels like He is not answering your prayers. You start to wonder, does God know I'm hurting? If so, then why doesn't He answer me? The answer here can be complicated to ascertain, but I have a few suggestions for you.

First, look for sin in your life—any sin. These are usually big ones like not being obedient to Him. For example, maybe you are living with your girlfriend and still having sex outside of marriage, which is something God forbids you to do. Now, if you are unwilling to obey Him, then why would He answer your prayer? That is not to say He can't or He won't. It may be that He is delaying His answer to your prayer because He wants you to pay attention to the sin in your life and be as repulsed by it as He is. Your first and foremost desire should be for your relationship with Him, and to do everything in your power to maintain that relationship. You must passionately desire to be obedient to Him. Perhaps He is just trying to teach you that lesson or make you aware of how important that is.

Second, He may be trying to grow you in the area of learning to trust Him. Trusting God is easy when things are going well. However, trusting Him becomes tremendously more difficult when we are struggling. When we are in the middle of a trial, God may be delaying His answer to your prayer because He wants to see if what you say, "I trust Him," is true. Now, God knows whether this is true or not, but you may not know it is true. The only way for Him to validate this for you is to set your life on fire a little. Maybe not a three-alarm fire, but a little brush fire here or there. Will you trust Him in and through the fire?

I did not do very well on this test. When my first special needs son was born, a small brush fire broke out in my life. I kind of, sort of, dealt with that, but not confidently. I left it smoldering on the side. When my second special needs son was born, the smoldering fire from my first son broke out all around me in flames. I chose anger towards God over trust. Take my advice: that is NEVER the correct choice!

Third, He may want you to walk through this struggle. Notice I said "walk" through it; do not live in it! Sometimes, He doesn't take us out of a struggle but walks with us through a struggle. A good example of this would be Pastor Greg Laurie of Harvest Christian Fellowship in Riverside, California and his wife, Cathe, when they lost their son Christopher in a tragic car accident on July 24, 2008. Unless you have gone through something like this, you cannot fathom the pain of losing a loved one, especially a child. Pastor Greg and Cathe faithfully serve God's Kingdom. Why would a loving God allow their son to die? I'm not God, so I do not know the answer to this question, but I do know who God is. He is loving, He is kind, He is holy, He is sovereign, He is righteous, and so much more. Because He is all these things, I can trust that He knows what He's doing. Greg and Cathe gave us an example by living it. Their hearts were not just broken; they were shattered. But they walked with Him through it. Through the hurt, through the pain, through the challenge of understanding. There was no way over it, around it, or under it. The only way for them to go was through it with God. To be honest, I have no idea how someone can go through something like that without Him.

When we walk with Him through these challenges, through these struggles, we can then see Him do some amazing things, not only in our lives but also in other people's lives and for His Kingdom. I'm sure Greg and Cathe would love to have their son back; I know I would love to have two "healthy" boys rather than two boys with special needs. However, if I ask myself honestly if I would trade what God has done in my life, my boys' lives, and all the other lives they have touched, for them to be "healthy," I would honestly say, "No, I would not." Why would I exchange a known entity for an unknown one? Besides, there is more of eternity with them being healthy than this brief period where they are disabled.

Finally, you may be asking the question incorrectly. Like I said in a previous chapter, your first clue to this will always be the word "why." If you are asking Him why, I can almost guarantee you are asking the wrong question. Again, instead of asking Him why, ask Him "what" and "how." These are the same questions you have seen several times now, 'What are you trying to teach me in this?" and "How do you want me to respond to this?" These questions are so much better for you than "why."

Sincere questions mean you are genuinely interested in knowing God's truth. Understand, this doesn't mean you will like His truth or even agree with His truth. It does mean that when you are sincere, you will accept His truth and adopt it as your own when He reveals it to you, regardless of what you, the world, or anyone else thinks. If for some reason you do not do this, or you refuse to do this, then your very act of refusal confirms your hypocrisy and insincerity.

I'm sorry. I know that is a strong statement, and the last thing I want to do is offend people. However, if you are unwilling to accept and adopt His truth as your own, then what will that say about your relationship with Him? You see, how you respond to God and to His truth has everything to do with your relationship with Him.

Perspective #56: How you respond to God and to His truth has everything to do with your relationship with Him.

Cooperate with Him, partner with Him and then see what He can do with your life and in your life as you fall more and more in love with Him.

Insincere questions like, "Can God create a boulder that is too big for Him to lift?" display an ignorance of who God is. They are mainly designed to show God is not all powerful because, one, He can't create something that is too big for Him to lift or two, that if He can, then He's not strong enough to lift it. Neither of which is true. The answer is God can do anything He desires to do. Nevertheless, the question doesn't matter either way. These types of questions reveal our ignorance of who He is and really shouldn't be asked. God can see our hearts and our motives. If we come to Him with a sincere heart, He will go out of His way to answer our questions.

Perspective #57: God can see our hearts and our motives. If we come to Him with a sincere heart, He will go out of His way to answer our questions.

He may do this by pointing us to the section of the Bible that answers our question. He may show us a book to read that answers our question or bring someone along to help give us the answer. He may put the answer in our daily devotional reading, or allow our Pastor to answer the question for us in his next message.

I am always amazed when I ask God a question, and within days, He answers it for me. I know this is a silly example, but let me show you what I mean.

One time, I was playing the California Lottery a little—a dollar here, two dollars there, not much. For some reason, I got sucked into the idea that God might want to bless me through the California Lottery (don't judge me!). Eventually, I started playing five dollars at a time, you know, to help God out a little (as if He needed my help). Then ten dollars, finally getting up to twenty dollars. Since the Lottery draws twice weekly, this was quickly becoming an expensive habit. Of course, I had very little to show for my investment.

I decided to ask God if this was okay by saying something like, "God, if you don't want me doing this, just let me know." Of course, I did not seriously expect Him to answer. I'm not sure I wanted Him to answer.

The very next Sunday morning, within the first five minutes of my pastor's message, he said something like, "Don't you all know that the Lottery is just a tax on STUPID!" I couldn't help but laugh. I was floored that God responded so quickly. It worked; I have not played the

Lottery since. The answer was enough to change my perspective and my desire.

Now, for all of you gambling aficionados, this isn't an indictment on the Lottery or gambling. If God hasn't told you that these things are just a tax on stupid, by all means, continue. However, if He has or is, then you may want to take it up with Him!

Finally, here's some biblical wisdom concerning insincere questions:

> *A scoffer seeks wisdom in vain, but knowledge is easy for a man of understanding. – Proverbs 14:6*

If you come to God with an insincere heart, He will know. And good luck on finding anything out. In the end, you may just look like a fool. However, come to God sincerely wanting to know Him and His truth, and that is when you will begin to find it. They call this wisdom! Understand, God is not a genie in a bottle who will perform for you anytime you demand it as if you can "make" Him do something.

Perspective #58: God is not a genie in a bottle who will perform for you anytime you demand it as if you can "make" Him do something.

Some people try to tempt God by saying things like, "God, if you exist, then give me a new car right now!" Of course, when the new car doesn't appear out of thin air, they say something stupid like, "Well, I guess God doesn't exist then," as if God's existence depended on Him performing some selfish, self-centered circus act for them. People like this do not "get" God, nor do they care to. Because He is all-powerful, God can and will make everyone stand before Him and give an account of their life.

Perspective #59: Because He is all-powerful, God can and will make everyone stand before Him and give an account of their life.

The truth we need to understand here is that we are all powerless to resist this future event. In the end, it doesn't matter whether you believe in Him or not; God will still hold you accountable, regardless of whether you *want* to be accountable. That's the cool thing about being all-powerful. Because He is all-powerful, God doesn't have to prove Himself on demand for your amusement!

Perspective #60: Because He is all-powerful, God doesn't have to prove Himself on demand for your amusement!

Joshua, who took over for Moses, said it best:

Now therefore fear the Lord and serve him in sincerity and in faithfulness. Put away the gods that your fathers served beyond the River and in Egypt, and serve the Lord. – Joshua 24:14

When you get the fact that God is all-powerful and all-knowing, you understand that He's going to know whether you are sincere or not. You can't fool someone who knows everything, so do not even try.

Of course, having the question is only part of the puzzle. Listening for the answer and desiring to learn can also be a challenge for us.

Perspective Recap:

- **Perspective #52:** "Never argue with a fool in public. Nobody knows who the fool is!" – Maureen Rose Plein
- **Perspective #53:** "Never argue with a fool in public. They will drag you down to their level and then beat you with experience." – Mark Twain
- **Perspective #54:** God will not hold you accountable for what someone else says about Him; He will only hold you accountable for what you believe is true.
- **Perspective #55:** God is excited to teach you, to grow you and to guide you! His passion and His desire is to help you fall more in love with Him and with who He is!
- **Perspective #56:** How you respond to God, and His truth has everything to do with your relationship with Him.
- **Perspective #57:** God can see our hearts and our motives. If we come to Him with a sincere heart, He will go out of His way to answer our questions.
- **Perspective #58:** God is not a genie in a bottle who will perform for you anytime you demand it as if you can "make" Him do something.
- **Perspective #59:** Because He is all-powerful, God can and will make everyone stand before Him and give an account of their life.
- **Perspective #60:** Because He is all-powerful, God doesn't have to prove Himself on demand for your amusement!

Seven: Learning Engines

One of the fascinating things I've discovered is that human beings are learning engines. We are designed to learn. Compelled by some unknown force to learn, we desire to learn, and we feel bored when we are not learning. Learning comes naturally to us, maybe by design.

Take, for example, a baby learning to walk. They try and fail, then they try again and fail some more. Some people come along and give them some assistance, and it helps, but they want to do it on their own. There's a sense of expected freedom in it for them, so they continue to try and fail, try some more and fail some more, until one day, they take a step and then another and, just like that, they've got it! They are walking, and everyone around is cheering. They are big stuff, they are amazing, and oops they fall again! Not to worry, they continue to try. Sure, they may take a break for a few days, but something is driving them to learn how to do this walking thing. After all, those big, tall people seem to be doing it with no problem; I should be able to do it as well. They continue to try, and before long, walking comes naturally.

How did this child learn to walk? Did mom and dad give them a bunch of instructions like, "Put one foot in front of the other, slowly keep your balance as you move from one foot, to the other, and whatever you do, do not fall. Falling is a failure, and there are no failures in this family!" Maybe, but how well do you think that worked out for them when the child barely understands the language they are speaking? My point exactly.

Children are driven to learn. Some mysterious force within them compels them to learn. Sure, they make a ton of mistakes, some people might call those mistakes failures, but they overcame them by not giving up. By not quitting. Through perseverance. They eventually learn how to do it, and the more they do it, the better they get at it. Practice does have an impact on how good we get at something.

I know this is an elementary example, but it quickly proves my point. We are driven to learn, to figure things out, to comprehend, and to understand. Eventually, we succeed and move onto the next challenge, learning to run or learning that you do not put pointy metal things in electrical outlets. Learning that you do not touch something when mom and dad say, "Don't touch that, it's HOT!" Life is full of lessons to be learned.

What would happen if the child in my example gave up and quit? Would they ever learn how to walk? Probably not. However, because they kept trying, they eventually learned. They discovered a way that worked. Sure, it's a little unstable at first, but it worked. With a bit more time and effort, they perfect it, and that's when it dawns on you, "Um, why did I encourage them to learn how to do this walking thing?" Now you are chasing them all over the house. Nothing is safe, everything is theirs, and you are not only exhausted after just 10 minutes of chasing them around the house, but you also realize everything you once owned is now THEIRS because the only word they seem to know is MINE!

We have been designed by God to learn, grow and discover all the intricate things about Him and His creation that He has made available to us.

Perspective #61: We have been designed by God to learn, grow, and discover all the intricate things about Him and His creation that He has made available to us.

When we want to know something, learning is fun, even exciting. Asking questions is an integral part of the learning process. This, of course, is by design. God created us to be this way. Since He created everything else and put it there for our pleasure and enjoyment, for us to discover, He needed a way to help us want to get to know Him and His creation more. What better way to accomplish this than to give us a passion, desire, a drive, a joy in learning new things? And a critical component of this learning process is asking sincere questions!

As we grow and mature, the questions and the lessons become more and more difficult. The minute we finish one lesson, there are ten more in line to take its place. Learning can be challenging, learning can be frustrating, and learning means failure. Most people do not realize that learning is a lifelong process of growing in our relationship with God, cooperating with Him, and partnering with Him!

Perspective #62: Learning is a lifelong process of growing in our relationship with God, cooperating with Him, and partnering with Him!

A significant part of learning is failing. That's right, failure and learning go together. We often see failure as a dreaded evil. We may even fear it. However, just think about what you could accomplish if your perspective was different. What if you looked at failure as a learning opportunity instead? What if you figured out how to leverage the failure to learn, to grow, and to become even better? Look at the example of the baby learning to walk; how did the baby learn? By doing, by exercising its muscles, by trying different things, by failing a lot! By using what worked and throwing away what didn't. We can learn a lot from this example. Understand, the purpose isn't to fail a lot; the purpose is to look for the best way to succeed, of which failure is an integral part. Failures are the stepping stones to success! Do not waste the failure; learn from it, grow from it, and use it to become a success!

Perspective #63: Failures are the stepping stones to success! Do not waste the failure; learn from it, grow from it, and use it to become a success!

Most people don't like to focus on failure. Failure is not fun. I'm sure the baby cried a few times when they were learning to walk and fell or bumped into something they didn't know how to get around. However, if you LEARN from the failure, what worked, what didn't work, and if you apply those lessons to your next attempt, it is no longer a failure; it is a learning exercise! You see, perspective!

My wife, Diana, and I met over 14 years ago. At the time, her daughters (Britney and Nicole), now ours, were 13 and 16. Several years ago, my wife showed me several of our daughter's baby videos. In one of them, our daughter Britney is just learning to walk. She must have been around 10 or 11 months old. Diana is behind the camera filming, talking to Britney. Nicole is sitting on the couch watching. Britney is smiling and laughing. Britney takes off walking, and for some reason, the oak coffee table in front of her didn't move out of her way, and "SMACK" goes the forehead onto the edge of the coffee table. Diana, on camera, nonchalantly says, "Oh, baby fall and go boom?" Britney, of course, gets up, looks a little stunned, then laughs and continues marching on. Me, I'm watching this, incredulous at my wife, the woman I thought walked on water, being so callous to the daughter I love! How dare she! "WHAT is the matter with you? You are so MEAN!" (Of course, I say this out loud.)

Now because I have two boys with special needs, I have never been through this parenting phase. Diana explained that if you don't overreact, they won't. This was a simple equation of life. I'm still traumatized, by the way; I still check Britney's forehead for scar damage!

I'm sure you have heard the story about Thomas Edison trying and failing an extraordinary number of times to make a light bulb, something we take for granted today. In my research, I found statements where they say he failed anywhere from 1,000 to 10,000 times. For this example, let's use 1,000 as the number of failures before he got it right. What if Thomas Edison gave up after 500 tries, or 750 tries, or even 999 tries? Thomas Edison would have never experienced success. The only way to truly fail is to give up and quit—to throw your toys out the window and walk off the playing field!

Perspective #64: The only way to truly fail is to give up and quit—to throw your toys out the window and walk off the playing field!

This is a critical perspective on your relationship with God. Understand, you are "finite," He is "infinite," and there is no way for you to comprehend Him and His ways fully. You currently cannot do so. Do not get discouraged if you run into a question you can't find an answer to, or a concept about Him that seems too difficult to grasp. Keep investing in your relationship with Him, try it again. Ask the question a different way. Get to know Him better, keep falling more and more in love with Him. Keep at it and never give up on Him and your relationship with Him. Ensure your success!

What you will find is that the more you know God, the easier the answers come to the difficult questions. You can then compare the question to what you know about Him. This is when you can put into perspective the difficult questions like "Why does God allow evil to exist?" and compare them to who you know God to be.

Since we know God hates evil, we know evil is not something He wants to tolerate. We also know He has given us the power to choose, which means that for Him to be just, He has given us the freedom to choose even if He doesn't agree with or like our choice. So, if we choose evil, He has to accept our choice. We can see that God isn't allowing evil; He is giving us the freedom to choose good vs. evil. Some of us choose evil, and as we'll learn more in the next book, all choice has consequences.

Also, do not make a mistake and put your focus on the wrong thing. Do not focus on what you don't know about God; instead, focus on what you DO know about God.

Perspective #65: Do not focus on what you don't know about God; instead, focus on what you DO know about God.

Far too often, people get hung up on the trivial things, and they allow those small obstacles to derail their relationship with God. This is because they are focusing on the wrong thing. They get hung up on what they do not know, what they can't understand, rather than trusting in what they do know, what they do understand. Sometimes, you have to accept the fact that you do not know something right now, which doesn't mean you won't know it in the future, but for now, it is an unknown to you. Accept it and move on. Embrace what you do know about God and quit dwelling on what you don't know.

Perspective #66: Embrace what you do know about God and quit dwelling on what you don't know.

We have a BIG God and small minds; we are not capable of knowing everything there is to know about God.

Perspective #67: We have a BIG God and small minds; we are not capable of knowing everything there is to know about God.

When we learn, we are accomplishing what God has intended for us. Since learning is an accomplishment, learning is rewarding. But how many times is success achieved on the first try? Rarely, if ever. If these examples I've been using teach us one thing, that would be, success is a process of repeated learning (a. k. a. failure) until you get it right.

Perspective #68: Success is a process of repeated learning (a.k.a. failure) until you get it right.

For some of us, as we get older and leave school or military service, we tend not to value learning as much as we did when we were younger. We stop growing, stop discovering, and thus our drive and ambition for learning seem to fall off a little. Maybe we become afraid of failure, and we stop trying. We quit learning. We are no longer exercising our ability to learn. Perhaps we think we know it all and do not feel the need to learn anymore, which is usually a phase we go through during adolescence; however, it can sometimes infect adults!

There are some of you out there who have never had this problem; you are always excited about learning new things. All I can say is, I'm jealous. I wish I had been that way.

I do not want to give the impression that I stopped learning altogether. For my job, as a computer programmer and eventually as a director of I.T., I am always learning new things. It is fun; I am having a blast, but because it is for my job, I never really considered it learning. Looking back, I realize I didn't have a problem learning new things about my job, but I invested little or no effort in learning new things about God. Sure, part of that reason could have been that I was mad at Him. Why would I want to learn anything new about someone that had nothing better to do than pick on me? Nevertheless, can you imagine the impact I could have had for His Kingdom if I applied myself to learning more about Him when I was younger?

For example, reading is one of many ways to learn, and for me, I've always hated reading. It's so time-consuming, and to be honest, I'm a slow reader. I need to make sure I'm comprehending and understanding what I'm reading, so I may read and re-read a paragraph several times before I get it. Let me clarify something before I finish my story. There is a reason I hate reading. Let me explain why.

When I was in high school, I heard rumors about college teachers saying something like, "Read these 300 pages from this book and these 250 pages from this other book and then write me a comparison report contrasting the differences between the two opinions presented. Your report needs to be 5,000 words, double-spaced, and it is due at the beginning of next week's class." To me, this isn't teaching; it is more like punishment, but I digress. By the way and for the record, I love teachers; my church is full of them I know none of them would EVER be that mean!

The fact that I'm a slow reader and need to comprehend and understand everything I read made this a terrifying obstacle to me. Being gripped by fear, college didn't sound nearly as much fun as playing war games in the Marine Corps.

Unbeknownst to me at the time, reading can also be fun. The stories you can involve yourself in, the places you can go, and the things you can learn are unimaginable. Nevertheless, because it required me to sit alone and do nothing but read, I did not perceive its tremendous value.

Enter the iPhone, iTunes, and Audible. I got my first iPhone in 2011 (I know, I was a late bloomer) and by the end of that year, I was starting to learn how to leverage it. I purchased Pastor Skip Heitzig's 729 series. This is 729 messages he's given over the years that takes you through the entire Bible, book by book. An entire Bible Study on mp3, how cool is that? Anyway, I started listening to that as I went out for my daily walk and found that I was learning as I was exercising. What a concept! So, I expanded this to listen on my drive to and from work, while I was outside working in the yard, or working on the piles of "honey do's" I had on my list.

It was AWESOME. I couldn't believe the wisdom I was absorbing while doing the things I did all the time. I learned so much from Skip's teachings that I couldn't get enough. It was like flipping a light switch. I had found a way to learn that didn't overwhelm me. So much so that I finished all 729 messages in less than 14 months.

After this, I ran into some relationship problems with another manager at work. I'd been working as a project manager for a regional grocery retail chain for three years and loved my job. Suddenly, I couldn't do anything right. It was like going from hero to zero overnight. It left me feeling dumbfounded as to what I had done wrong.

I figured I must be doing something wrong relationally. When researching what to do and how to fix my problem, I kept running across this book called *How to Win Friends and Influence People* by Dale Carnegie. At the time, this book was 65 years old, and I was pretty sure it wasn't going to help me with a modern-day problem. However, I'm not sure why I did, but I decided to give it a try. What could it hurt? I opened an Audible account and downloaded the *How to Win Friends and Influence People* audiobook to my iPhone and started listening.

This was amazing! There was so much wisdom in this one book that I read (listened to), so I listened to it two more times. Then the thought occurred to me, "What if there are more books out there with just as much wisdom in them?" So, I downloaded several other books that were recommended by others and was on the fast track to audio learning.

If you love sitting down with a book and turning the pages or using a digital reader, that is a wonderful thing. I applaud you and might even be a little jealous. However, for those of us who are challenged by that process, we have another option.

The point I want to make with this is that there are no excuses for you NOT to learn. YOU have been designed and empowered with the ability to learn new and amazing things. Please visit my website WalkerJamesAuthor.com and the "Resources" tab to see a list of books I recommend you read and why. There are some terrific books out there and some fantastic authors God has blessed with the ability to communicate Him to the rest of us.

Remember Perspective #11: "God will hold you accountable for all the evidence of His existence regardless of whether you believe it or not." Cooperate with God, partner with God to learn as much about Him as you can and to serve His Kingdom.

The amount of content for you to learn from, listen to, read and absorb is staggering. There is no excuse for not doing so. Remember to always learn with an open mind, first asking God, "What is it you want me to learn? Give me the wisdom to see your truth and help me to retain what I read and what I learn and apply it to my life." When you do this, you begin to cooperate with God's design for you and for your life. You find out more about Him and this magnificent world He created. This, in turn, empowers you to serve Him and His Kingdom better. Be sure to always compare what other people say to what the Bible says about God; that way, you will always be able to discern His truth!

Perspective #69: Be sure to always compare what other people say to what the Bible says about God; that way, you will always be able to discern His truth!

Ask Him all the time, ask Him everything! Ask Him when you do not know and when you do not understand. Ask Him when you are struggling with the why. Ask Him for job advice. Ask Him for relationship advice. If someone says something about Him that doesn't quite sound right, run it by Him and seek His truth. Even things that seem plausible, still run them by Him. Ask Him! Since God wants a close, personal, loving, intimate relationship with you, then He positively wants you to ASK Him everything.

Perspective #70: Since God wants a close, personal, loving, intimate relationship with you, then He positively wants you to ASK Him everything.

In the New Testament, Jesus' brother James says it so much better than I can:

If any of you lacks wisdom, let him ask God, who gives generously to all without reproach, and it will be given him. – James 1:5

You see, God wants you to pursue this relationship with Him. If this relationship wasn't something you could invest in, then why did Jesus say:

> *Ask, and it will be given to you; seek, and you will find; knock, and it will be opened to you. For everyone who asks receives, and the one who seeks finds, and to the one who knocks it will be opened. – Matthew 7:7-8*

God is giving abundantly to those asking, to those seeking, to those knocking. Jesus goes on to explain that if we, as sinful human beings, know how to give good gifts to our children, how much more will His perfect, righteous and holy Father give to you if you just ask?

> *Or which one of you, if his son asks him for bread, will give him a stone? Or if he asks for a fish, will give him a serpent? If you then, who are evil, know how to give good gifts to your children, how much more will your Father who is in heaven give good things to those who ask him! – Matthew 7:9-11*

Do not be afraid to ask God anything and everything; your sincere questions only stoke the fires of your learning engine and can only enhance and grow your relationship with Him.

Perspective #71: Your sincere questions only stoke the fires of your learning engine and can only enhance and grow your relationship with God.

Perspective Recap:

- **Perspective #61:** We are designed by God to learn, grow, and discover all the intricate things about Him and His creation that He has made available to us.

- **Perspective #62:** Learning is a lifelong process of growing in our relationship with God, cooperating with Him, partnering with Him.

- **Perspective #63:** Failures are the stepping stones to success! Do not waste the failure; learn from it, grow from it, and use it to become a success!

- **Perspective #64:** The only way to truly fail is to give up and quit—to throw your toys out the window and walk off the playing field!

- **Perspective #65:** Do not focus on what you don't know about God; instead, focus on what you DO know about God!

- **Perspective #66:** Embrace what you do know about God and quit dwelling on what you don't know.

- **Perspective #67:** We have a BIG God and small minds; we are not capable of knowing everything there is to know about God.

- **Perspective #68:** Success is a process of repeated learning (a.k.a. failure) until you get it right.

- **Perspective #69:** Be sure to always compare what other people say to what the Bible says about God; that way, you will always be able to discern His truth!

- **Perspective #70:** Since God wants a close, personal, loving, intimate relationship with you, then He positively wants you to ASK Him everything.

- **Perspective #71:** Your sincere questions only stoke the fires of your learning engine and can only enhance and grow your relationship with God.

Eight: What about Doubt?

Doubt is the feeling of uncertainty or the lack of conviction. Doubt for the disciple of Jesus Christ is being unsure of what you believe and why. Doubt is not unbelief; however, it can become unbelief if unattended. As we saw with the Apostle Thomas, doubt can sometimes be a refusal to believe. Thomas refused to accept that Jesus had risen from the dead until he touched the wounds in His hands and the wound in His side.

> *Now Thomas, one of the twelve, called the Twin,[11] was not with them when Jesus came. So, the other disciples told him, "We have seen the Lord." But he said to them, "Unless I see in his hands the mark of the nails, and place my finger into the mark of the nails, and place my hand into his side, I will never believe."*
>
> *Eight days later, his disciples were inside again, and Thomas was with them. Although the doors were locked, Jesus came and stood among them and said, "Peace be with you." Then he said to Thomas, "Put your finger here, and see my hands; and put out your hand, and place it in my side. Do not disbelieve, but believe." Thomas answered him, "My Lord and my God!" Jesus said to him, "Have you believed because you have seen me? Blessed are those who have not seen and yet have believed." – John 20:24-29*

As you can see, not even the apostles, Jesus' closest friends, were immune to doubt. There was no reason for Thomas to disbelieve the words of the other apostles. They had no reason to lie to him. But he demanded physical proof.

In the case of Thomas, Jesus kindly gave him the proof he was seeking. However, for you and me, He does not always do so. Can you

---

[11] Some translations use Thomas (Aramaic) and some use Didymus (Greek) - both mean twin.

imagine seven billion people all demanding for Jesus to appear to them so they can touch the nail prints in His hands and the wound in His side before they will believe in Him? For Thomas, Jesus made an exception. For you and me, He may say, "I have given you more than enough evidence to believe. To choose not to is pure foolishness on your part!"

As C.S. Lewis points out in his book *The Screwtape Letters*, doubt is just a ploy Satan uses to get Christians to break their link with God. You see, faith is your link to God, your umbilical cord with God, so to speak, where He can empower you with His wisdom and grace.

Perspective #72: Faith is your link to God, your umbilical cord with God, so to speak, where He can empower you with His wisdom and grace.

Doubt chips away at faith, and if not addressed right away, it can destroy it. When you let doubt creep in, and you do not face it head-on, it can and will destroy your faith, destroy your relationship with God. I do not say this to scare you. On the contrary, I say this to encourage you to see doubt as okay. It is an integral part of your walk with God; you just can't leave it unattended.

We often allow doubt to creep into our lives when we do not have all the answers. Because we do not know, we feel there is no way to know. This doubt, of course, is the furthest thing from the truth, and that is why I discussed questions and learning before I started discussing doubt. Asking questions, researching answers, and investing in learning are just some tools you have at your disposal to combat doubt. The question is, will you use them?

Giving into doubt is violating two perspectives we discussed earlier. Perspective #64: "The only way to truly fail is to give up and quit—to throw your toys out the window and walk off the playing field." And Perspective #65: "Do not focus on what you don't know about God; instead, focus on what you DO know about God!"

Adopting both perspectives is critical in your fight against doubt. Just because you do not know, doesn't mean it can't be known, so don't give up. Keep praying and asking God for the answers; He will bring them to you when you are ready to receive them.

It is important for you to understand you are a finite creature. There is NO WAY for you to know everything about an infinite God, so quit trying! Take your focus off what you do not know and put it back on what you do know about God. I have tripped myself up so many times on this one. I give into fear, worry, and doubt because I do not know something. I can't tell you how many times God has had to remind me of this fact.

Have you seen the Disney/Pixar movie *Up*? I love this movie, and I love Dug. He's the loveable dog that Carl and Russell run into on their adventure. During one of the scenes, Dug loses his focus in the middle of a conversation and cries out "squirrel," as if he wanted to go chase after it or something. That is precisely what doubt is. It is a squirrel; don't chase it. Do not give into doubt and take your focus off who you know God to be and put it on something you do not know for sure. This doesn't mean you don't invest time and effort to resolve your doubts, to answer those questions. It just means you do not focus on your doubts. Instead, you keep your focus on Him. It is okay to admit you do not know something.

Understand, the enemy can't interfere with your relationship with God if you keep your focus on Him, where it belongs. That is why he has carefully crafted a lot of doubt so he can suck you in and get you to take your focus off where it needs to be: on God Himself. There are a lot of people out there who are trapped by doubt and can't seem to get out of it. That is because they allow the enemy to keep them focused on it, in bondage to it. That is why you will become what you focus on.

Perspective #73: You will become what you focus on.

If you focus on doubt, you will become even more doubtful. If you focus on God, you will become godlier. It's a simple equation that has helped me many times.

To deal with doubt, first, you need to pray and ask God for the wisdom to address your doubts properly to not be afraid of them, but to allow them to drive you to find out the answers. To allow you to draw closer to Him for the answers. If you are sincerely seeking His truth, God is not one to play hide and seek with it. He wants you to know, and He wants to reveal it to you. However, if you are not sincere, then He may decide to keep the truth hidden from you. A perfect example of this is the cross of Jesus Christ as Paul points out in 1 Corinthians:

> *For the word of the cross is folly to those who are perishing, but to us who are being saved it is the power of God. For it is written, "I will destroy the wisdom of the wise, and the discernment of the discerning I will thwart."[12] – 1 Corinthians 1:18-19*

People who do not want to get the cross of Jesus Christ won't. To them, it is just foolishness. They don't care about the hidden things of God, and they certainly won't invest the time and effort it takes to get to know Him. However, to those who are sincerely seeking the truth, God is overjoyed to reveal it to them.

Do not let the enemy use doubt to interfere with your relationship with God. Take the time to research and invest in your relationship with Him. Doing this work will turn your doubt into faith in no time, and you will grow in your relationship with God. Around every corner, you will be amazed at Him and who He is. The incredible part is that you have only scratched the surface; He is so much more than what we can discover here in these limited, frail bodies.

You say, "I still have doubts and questions." So what? So do I. Everyone has doubts and questions, so why shouldn't you? As a finite creature, you can't expect to understand everything about an infinite God and how He does things; Paul certainly didn't.

> *For who has known the mind of the Lord, or who has been his counselor? Or who has given a gift to him that he might be repaid? For from him and through him and to him are all things. To him be glory forever. Amen. – Romans 11:33-36*

Many of the Old Testament writers expressed doubts and even questioned God. Job is one of the biggest. There are 42 chapters in the

---

[12] See Isaiah 29:14.

book of Job, and if you have ever read it, you will notice that Chapters 1 – 37 are spent telling the story of Job and how he got into his situation. Several times Job cries out, "If I could only question God, then I could defend myself, and He would know my innocence" (paraphrase). Job is obviously frustrated with his situation and the fact that God is not answering him. Then, beginning in Chapter 38 and lasting a total of four chapters, God questions Job. He starts by asking Job, "Where were you when I laid the foundations of the earth?" I guess when God starts off asking you that question, you know you're in for a hard day. The cool thing about God sharing the story of Job with us is that we get to see just a glimpse of who He is, how big and mighty He is. It takes God four chapters to reveal this fantastic snippet; it is an excellent story, and when God is finished questioning Job, all Job can say is:

> I had heard of you by the hearing of the ear, but now my eye sees you; therefore, I despise myself, and repent in dust and ashes." – Job 42:5-6

One thing doubt causes us to do is to judge God and what He's doing or allowing to be done: a two-year-old child who develops cancer and dies before their third birthday; a 23-year-old who's in need of a kidney and has been on dialysis for six years; a close friend whose mother is in a nursing home suffering from dementia; parents whose son is born three months premature; brand-new parents who suddenly lose their two-month-old for no explainable reason; your father dies of a massive heart attack when you are seven. People may often respond to these tragedies just like I did when God gave me two boys with special needs. Why? What are you doing to me? Why are you picking on me? Don't you see my pain? Why? Why? Why?

Like I said earlier, why is not a good question to ask God. It doesn't build up and grow your relationship with Him. Instead, it usually has the opposite effect of destroying your relationship. Just like the "why" question, doubt, if unattended, is devastating to your relationship with God. Do not let it fester, do not let it get out of control. Accept that there is no way for you to know ALL things that can be known about God and that it is okay for you not to know some things.

Since we are finite creatures who must make our decisions based on probability, there has to be a point when we realize the weight of the evidence comes down on one side or the other. We'll never have all the answers, but there are more than enough clues to give God the benefit of our doubts.

Finally, have you ever thought about questioning your doubts? Just ask yourself, "Is it reasonable to doubt that Christianity is true considering all the evidence?" Probably not. The fact is that considering the evidence, you should have a lot more doubts about atheism and every other non-Christian belief system. They are not reasonable; Christianity is. Start doubting your doubts and accept Christ. It takes too much faith to believe anything else.[13]

---

[13] From the book, *I don't have enough Faith to be an Atheist* by Norm Geisler and Frank Turek.

Perspective Recap:

- **Perspective #72:** Faith is your link to God, your umbilical cord with God, so to speak, where He can empower you with His wisdom and grace.
- **Perspective #73:** You will become what you focus on.

Nine: Beautiful You

The world typically values people based on their outward beauty, personal wealth or something amazing they've accomplished. What if God did that? What if He only loved you if you were remarkably good looking? Only loved you if you had tons of money and were willing to give some of it to Him and His causes? Only loved you if you had first overcome astronomical odds to accomplish a great feat? What if God judged us like we judge each other? How terrible would that be?

Thankfully, God does things a little differently.

> *For there is one God, and there is one mediator between God and men, the man Christ Jesus, who gave himself as a **ransom** for all, which is the testimony given at the proper time. – 1 Timothy 2:5-6, emphasis added*

The key word in this Bible passage is "ransom," which can also be translated "redeem." In the first century, to "ransom" or "redeem" a slave meant to set them completely free. They owed nothing. You paid the price "in full" for their freedom. The simple fact that something of great value was exchanged as part of the transaction inferred that whatever was being "ransomed" or "redeemed" was extremely valuable or precious to the person paying the price.

God has paid a significant price for your freedom from sin and death. Understand, not just any price. Your freedom, your ransom, and your redemption from sin and death cost God everything. He gave His most precious gift, His most valued possession to save you!

Perspective #74: Your freedom, your ransom, and your redemption from sin and death cost God everything. He gave His most precious gift, His most valued possession to save you!

Also notice the Apostle Paul is clarifying to his protégé Timothy who this ransom was paid for when he says "who GAVE himself a

RANSOM for ALL." Jesus Christ GAVE Himself freely, paid the price FULLY, for ALL who accept His gift of Love! You, me, everyone!

Perspective #75: Jesus Christ GAVE Himself freely, paid the price FULLY, for ALL who accept His gift of love! You, me, everyone!

The Apostle Peter also talks about us being "ransomed" when he says:

---

*And if you call on him as Father who judges impartially according to each one's deeds, conduct yourselves with fear throughout the time of your exile, knowing that you were **ransomed** from the futile ways inherited from your forefathers, not with perishable things such as silver or gold, but with the precious blood of Christ, like that of a lamb without blemish or spot. – 1 Peter 1:17-19, emphasis added*

Read this passage slowly to get the deeper meaning. "Not with perishable things such as silver and gold (or money), but with the precious blood of Christ." God spared no expense to redeem you from sin and death.

Perspective #76: God spared no expense to redeem you from sin and death.

And if God spared no expense to ransom you, to redeem you, what does that say about how valuable, how precious you are to God?

Perspective #77: If God spared no expense to ransom you and to redeem you, what does that say about how valuable and precious you are to God?

You must be extremely valuable, extremely special, for God to go through so much trouble to ransom you, to redeem you! Well, let's see just how valuable, how precious you are to Him!

God gave His one and only Son, Jesus Christ, His most precious gift, His most valued possession, to die on the cross for your sins. Jesus took the judgment your sins deserved, the punishment you deserved for the sins you have committed. Jesus did this so nothing would stand in the way of your relationship with Him and His Father. Like I said, what does that say about God? He must think you're worth it for Him to sacrifice His Beloved Son for you. Because to save you, it cost Him everything He had. He did this because He thought you were worth it because He loves you dearly!

With your sin debt paid by Jesus Christ, you stand righteous before God, rather than as a sinner before God. God now sees you through His Son Jesus rather than seeing you as you are. He can do this because His Son led a perfect, sinless life and sacrificed Himself for you.

Also, you are holy. To be holy means you are "set apart for honorable use." This "holiness" has two components to it. The first is positional holiness within our relationship with God. We are holy because He is holy. He has set us apart to Himself. The second is practical holiness, which must be actively pursued within our relationship with Him. God expects us to cultivate a lifestyle of holiness by honoring Him in everything we do.

Therefore, preparing your minds for action, and being sober-minded, set your hope fully on the grace that will be brought to you at the revelation of Jesus Christ. As obedient children, do not be conformed to the passions of your former ignorance, but as he who called you is holy, you also be holy in all your conduct, since it is written, "You shall be holy, for I am holy." – 1 Peter 1:13-16

And here's the coolest part! You have been adopted into God's family as His child:

*In love he predestined us for **adoption** to himself as sons through Jesus Christ, according to the purpose of his will, to the praise of his glorious grace, with which he has blessed us in the Beloved. – Ephesians 1:5-6, emphasis added*

Since He is the King, what does that make you? That makes you a prince or a princess. And since there is no such thing as an ugly prince or princess, you are automatically beautiful! To sum all that up, if you have accepted Jesus as your Lord and Savior, you are a valuable, precious, pure, spotless, holy, beautiful prince or princess of the most high God!

Perspective #78: If you have accepted Jesus as your Lord and Savior, you are a valuable, precious, pure, spotless, holy, beautiful prince or princess of the most high God!

Wow! Aren't you something? Your challenge, should you choose to accept it, is to see yourself as God sees you. Study God's Word, and you will find out that you are precious, created in your mother's womb by God's very own hand. You are not an accident; you are not a mistake. Even if someone has told you this before or said they never wanted you, be assured, God has always wanted you.

Perspective #79: You are not an accident; you are not a mistake. Even if someone has told you this before or said they never wanted you, be assured, God has always wanted you.

If this were not so, God would never have spent so much to redeem you, to ransom you. Your salvation cost Him everything that was precious to Him. He thought you were worth the expense, the sacrifice, the pain, the suffering. You are truly special, you are truly worth it, and you are loved so deeply by Him. You ARE beautiful!

Jesus did not want to live in heaven without you, which is why He "chose" to die for you so that you could spend eternity with Him!

Perspective #80: Jesus did not want to live in heaven without you, which is why He "chose" to die for you so that you could spend eternity with Him!

Hillsong, who has generated some great Christian music in this past decade, says this in a similar fashion in their song *What a Beautiful Name* when they sing:

> You didn't want heaven without us
> So Jesus, You brought heaven down
> My sin was great, Your love was greater
> What could separate us now

You see, it's all about your relationship with Him. That is what He wants. He is just waiting for you to want it as well. And here is why God did this:

For the grace of God has appeared, bringing salvation for all people, training us to renounce ungodliness and worldly passions, and to live self-controlled, upright, and godly lives in the present age, waiting for our blessed hope, the appearing of the glory of our great God and Savior Jesus Christ, who gave himself for us to redeem us from all lawlessness and to purify for himself a people for his own possession who are zealous for good works.
– Titus 2:11-14

He wants you to be like Him and be "zealous" (enthusiastic, passionate, fervent) for good works!

You might say, "Well, I don't feel valuable or worthwhile." The only problem with feelings is that they sometimes lie to us. The fact is, you are valuable, you have great worth, you are gifted, you are talented, and you have a purpose on earth. God has more than proven this. Your choice will always be, do I believe my feelings, or do I believe the facts that I know about God?

A good friend of mine made a wonderful point recently when he said, "God's love for you does not have a beginning; it never started. He has always loved you!"

Perspective #81: "God's love for you does not have a beginning; it never started. He has always loved you!" – Brad Camp

This perspective of ourselves is essential to keep the enemy, our thoughts and are feelings from pummeling us with lies. My pastor and friend added to my insight on this just the other day when in his Sunday message, he gave me this perspective. What other people think about you is NONE of YOUR business. Focus on what God thinks about you and your relationship with Him. That is YOUR business.

Perspective #82: "What other people think about you is NONE of YOUR business. Focus on what God thinks about you and your relationship with Him. That is YOUR business." – Pastor Ron Wood

The world is full of "naysayers," people who have nothing better than to tell you "you can't," "you're not good enough," or "you're stupid for believing in that Jesus character." The key for you is deciding whom you will listen. Them or God? The question you need to ask anyone who discourages you from pursuing a relationship with God is, "How far would you go to have a relationship with me? Would you go as far as God went?"

Perspective #83: The question you need to ask anyone who discourages you from pursuing a relationship with God is, "How far would you go to have a relationship with me? Would you go as far as God went?"

Would they die for you? What if they knew all about you and your "secret" sins; would they still die for you? It would be hard to find anyone to take this deal, but God did! God didn't HAVE to do what He did, but because of your need and my need, He chose to do it.

Perspective #84: God didn't HAVE to do what He did, but because of your need and my need, He chose to do it.

You must have enormous value to Him. You must have enormous worth to Him. Which means, even though God doesn't need a relationship with you, He wants a relationship with you.

Perspective #85: Even though God doesn't need a relationship with you, He wants a relationship with you.

How amazing is that? God wants this relationship with you.

---

*The Lord your God is in your midst, a mighty one who will save; he will **rejoice** over you with gladness; he will quiet you by his love; he will exult over you with loud singing.*
– Zephaniah 3:17, emphasis added

This says that God is going to "rejoice over you with gladness; he will quiet you by his love; he will exult (gloat) over you with loud singing." If God is going to do that for you, why listen to the world? Why take your perspective, your self-worth from what they say? The question will never be, does God love you? Does God want you? Does God want a relationship with you? The question will always come down to, do you want a relationship with Him? Bottom line, the choice is always yours, so choose wisely!

- **Perspective #74:** Your freedom, your ransom, and your redemption from sin and death cost God everything. He gave His most precious gift, His most valued possession to save you!

- **Perspective #75:** Jesus Christ GAVE Himself freely, paid the price FULLY, for ALL who accept His gift of love! You, me, everyone!

- **Perspective #76:** God spared no expense to redeem you from sin and death!

- **Perspective #77:** If God spared no expense to ransom you and to redeem you, what does that say about how valuable and precious you are to God?

- **Perspective #78:** If you have accepted Jesus as your Lord and Savior, you are a valuable, precious, pure, spotless, holy, beautiful prince or princess of the most high God!

- **Perspective #79:** You are not an accident; you are not a mistake. Even if someone has told you this before or said they never wanted you, be assured, God has always wanted you.

- **Perspective #80:** Jesus did not want to live in heaven without you, which is why He chose to die for you so that you could spend eternity with Him!

- **Perspective #81:** "God's love for you does not have a beginning; it never started. He has always loved you!" – Brad Camp

- **Perspective #82:** "What other people think about you is NONE of YOUR business. Focus on what God thinks about you and your relationship with Him. That is YOUR business." – Pastor Ron Wood

- **Perspective #83:** The question you need to ask anyone who discourages you from pursuing a relationship with God is, "How far would you go to have a relationship with me? Would you go as far as God went?"

- **Perspective #84:** God didn't HAVE to do what He did, but because of your need and my need, He chose to do it.

- **Perspective #85:** Even though God doesn't need a relationship with you, He wants a relationship with you.

Ten: No Matter What

I still remember how adorable he was when he first arrived back in September 1968 to be my brother. He was one and a half years old when he, his father, and his older brother moved in with my mom, sister, three brothers and me. My mom and new stepfather had just gotten married. Now there were nine people—two parents and seven kids—all living in 1,200 square feet. It might have been a little crowded, but looking back, I'm not sure I would have had it any other way. At the time, we were a family!

My sister, brothers, and I had just lost our father in January of that year due to a massive heart attack. Lowell, and his brother had just lost their mother around the same time from a severe infection that took her life.

Lowell was the baby of the family. He was the special, adorable one. I loved the way he looked up to me. The way he wanted to be just like me. The way he wanted to do everything I did, just because I did it. Not that I was anything special, but the fact that he thought I was, always meant the world to me.

When I was fourteen, Lowell was seven. Our father's employer was having a company picnic at Oxbow Park in Portland, Oregon, where we lived. We had just consumed about 20 hot-dogs and several sodas. But Lowell insisted we go on the Spider amusement park ride. I wasn't much of a fan of spinning, twirling, up, down, turn around until you puke rides, but Lowell, he could ride anything, and of course, he wanted to ride with me. Unfortunately for him, he didn't know the price he'd have to pay for that desire.

For those of you who don't know what the Spider is, it is an amusement park ride that has five main arms with two buckets for two people each at the end of each arm for a total of 10 pairs of riders. Its sole purpose is to go up and down and spin you around, slowly at first and then picking up speed. The faster it goes, the higher you go, and the more you turn and spin and jerk up and then down. It's a lot of fun (NOT). It lasts about three minutes, and I think that is about two minutes and fifty-nine seconds too long.

From the beginning, I didn't feel well. What I mean to say is that I started feeling queasy right away. It could have been all the food we consumed five minutes earlier, but I'm not sure, that is just speculation. I remember how proud Lowell was getting to ride with his older brother. I remember seeing Mom and Dad standing under the awning watching us kids ride, waving at us as we went around picking up speed. Two of my younger brothers were riding with us in another car.

We must have made about 4 or 5 spins around when it happened. Hot dog chunks just started spewing out of my mouth, and I couldn't stop it. I remember distinctly looking at them flying through the air and musing to myself, "Wow, those are barely digested chunks of hot-dog." I also remember looking at Lowell as I was spewing hot-dogs pieces around the park. I think he was trying to dodge the projectiles, not having much luck. There was a look of fear on his face, thinking he was going to get hit by some of them.

Lowell, stuck in this two-foot car with me, was trying to move as far away from me as he could. This may have been the only time I ever felt that Lowell no longer wanted to be with his "big brother." I think if he could have, he would have jumped out of the spinning, twirling, jerking, spider. The momentum of the ride combined with the spinning was tossing vomit all over the place and all over everyone. Especially Lowell and me. I believe we ended up with the brunt of the mess. However, I do recall seeing hot-dog chunks flying through the air and hitting bystanders on the ground.

As the ride slowed down to let us off, two of my younger brothers, Merit and Bobby, were in a car next to us. When the ride stopped, they got off first. Of course, one of them had to inform the operator of what he already knew. "That guy just threw up all over the place."

"I know," he said, slamming the door after they exited. I'm not sure he was too pleased with having to clean up the mess I had just made.

Lowell and I climbed out, covered in, well, you know, and we started wobbling over to Mom and Dad for some love and sympathy. This was the moment we found out that Mom and Dad's love was NOT unconditional! They started slowly backing away from us, hiding further under the awning and proceeded to disown us. They pointed to the car and said, "Go!" They didn't want us anywhere near them! They didn't care that we were traumatized and covered in puke and needing to be comforted. The only thing they cared about was not letting anyone see that "their" kid was the one throwing up on the amusement park ride.

The car ride home was painful, with nine people in a small Mazda station wagon, Lowell and I in the back because, well, we stunk and everyone else made sure we knew it for the 45-minute ride home.

You would think that would have changed the way Lowell looked at me, but it did not. As it was, I did not deserve his admiration. I let my brother Lowell down; I wasn't there to protect him from the abuse he received from my mother in retaliation for my father protecting him. Sure, none of us could pick on him anymore, but she could, and she was mean and vicious in her attacks on him!

As we grew older, I wasn't there to guide him and educate him about the dangers of alcohol and the risks of getting addicted to it. I never told him how damaging it could be to your life, your life choices, and all your relationships, including your relationship with your wife, your children and especially with God.

I wasn't there to guide him and educate him about the dangers of drugs and their even greater risks for getting addicted. I never told him how, if he started down that path, they would destroy his life and could put him into bondage to an addiction so strong it would rule over him and everything he did in the future. That it would cost him everything he valued, his job, his wife, his children, his family, his friends and eventually, his life.

No, I wasn't a very good brother to a young man who looked up to me, who admired me, and for that, I'm sorry, Lowell. I let you down.

My youngest brother, Lowell, went home to be with the Lord on September 17th, 2017. His struggle with heroin addiction finally is over. He is now at peace in His Kingdom with my fathers.

It's no secret, my brother Lowell was a sinner. In man's eyes, Lowell could have been considered a much worse sinner than me; however, in God's eyes (which is what matters), he was a sinner same as me. No better, no worse. The same!

You might be asking yourself right about now, how does this guy know that Lowell is even in Heaven? After all, we know how big of a sinner he was. The truth is that none of us are capable of judging anyone else. We are all sinners, every single one of us. Can one sinner adequately judge or condemn another sinner?

Perspective #86: We are all sinners, every single one of us. Can one sinner adequately judge or condemn another sinner?

The truth is that none of us has the wisdom or the purity to pronounce judgment on anyone else. Yet we do it all the time. I'm glad God doesn't care about or listen to the verdicts we so callously pronounce on others.

Lowell is in heaven for one reason and one reason only. He desired a relationship with God through Jesus Christ empowered by the Holy Spirit. I know this because the two of us had talked about it several times over the past 7 or 8 years. You see, Lowell and I spoke, or should I say, texted, several times a month. That is the special benefit you get when you pay for his cell phone; you get to talk to him and tell him you love him. You also get to hear about the pain he's in, how sad he is about all the mistakes he made, how much he loved his children, how ashamed he was because he let them down, and how hard it was to face them in his condition.

Here's the problem with sin, any sin, all sin: It is a trap. It is bondage, and it doesn't want to let you go. True, some sins are harder to break than others, but all sin is bondage. And if you know anything about sin, sin is what interferes with your relationship with God.

Perspective #87: If you know anything about sin, sin is what interferes with your relationship with God.

Now, here's the cool thing about God being all-knowing. He already knows you are a sinner. He already knows how "bad" of a sinner you are. In fact, He already knows about every sin you've ever committed, big or small, including the ones you've even forgotten.

God wants to meet you where you are, not where you think you should be, but exactly where you are. In the cesspool of your sin. Where you are, right here, right now, no conditions, no special consideration, no pre-cleaning required. Just a desire, on your part, to have a relationship with Him! That's it, that's all!

My brother Lowell was never able to break free from his bondage to sin or his addiction to heroin. His addictions had him locked down so tight for so long, that he could not break free physically; however, "relationally," He chose God! Understand, like me, Lowell continued to sin after he chose to enter into a relationship with God. Which begs the question, does our sin negate what God did? Not at all. You see, our salvation is never about what we can do; it is and always has been about what God has already done!

Perspective #88: Our salvation is never about what we can do; it is and always has been about what God has already done!

It is about what God did through His Son Jesus Christ on the cross almost 2,000 years ago. Understand, when you break free of one sin, there is always another one there to take its place. Let's face it; you will be a sinner until the day you die. There is no getting around this. And it doesn't matter whether these are big sins or little ones. So if, on this side of Heaven, you will ALWAYS be a sinner, how can anyone get to Heaven?

Quite simply, it is not about your sin; it is all about your relationship with God. Desire a relationship with God first; God will work with you over time to take care of the sin issues in your life. Just understand, you are never going to be "free from sin" until you die. This is not a "license" to sin; it is just a fact that you ARE a sinner. Only within a relationship with God can you successfully focus on doing good and refrain from doing evil.

Perspective #89: Only within a relationship with God can you successfully focus on doing good and refrain from doing evil.

Now, don't make a mistake and say, "Well, I only have little sins anymore." Understand, ALL sin, big, little and everything in-between is offensive to God. It doesn't matter to Him. What matters to Him is your passion, your desire for a relationship with Him. Ask Him to come into your heart. Tell Him you want a relationship with Him, desire to get to know Him and what He wants for you! Then ask Him to help you to see sin as offensively as He does.

When you do this, then and only then, you will start to focus on falling in love with Him more and sinning less. Because now, your relationship with God is what is driving your behavior. You do and don't do things because of your relationship with God. You choose not to sin because you know Him and how sin will interfere with your relationship with Him, and the last thing you want is for something to come in between you and Him.

I'm not sure if my brother Lowell realized this or not, but no matter what you do, say, think or don't do, God is ALWAYS going to love you! No matter what!

Perspective #90: No matter what you do, say, think or don't do, God is ALWAYS going to love you! No matter what!

Understand, God is never going to like your sin, but He is always going to love you!

Perspective #91: Understand, God is never going to like your sin, but He is always going to love you!

God's desire for a relationship with you will not change until the day you die. At that moment, your decision on whether YOU want a relationship with God is final. By this time, you will either surrender to Him and His will for your life or continue to rebel and defiantly shake your fist at Him. Either way, for you, His very next act will be His final act of love towards you. He will either say to you, "My son, my daughter, come into my house for all of eternity and enjoy your inheritance (which the best part is Him)," or, out of love, He's going to honor your desire to

NOT be with Him, to NOT have a relationship with Him. At this time, He will say to you, "As you wish, depart from me."

The only problem with this is that most of us don't realize what this truly means. We haven't taken the time to get to know God. When you know who He is, then you know the depth of the devastation of God saying to you, "Depart from me." What is happening with this statement is, God is saying, "I love you too much to dishonor your desire to NOT be with me. I have created a place for those who do not want to be with me."

Since God is all goodness, happiness, joy, love, peace, kindness and so much more, when you say NO to God, you are also saying NO to who and what He is. You are saying NO to all goodness, happiness, joy, love, peace, kindness and so much more because that is who He is! Since He is not going to be where He sends you because you want nothing to do with Him, you will not have those things as well, and that, my friend, is the worst part about saying NO to God.

Because you want nothing to do with Him, you want nothing to do with goodness. Because you want nothing to do with Him, you want nothing to do with happiness. Because you want nothing to do with Him, you want nothing to do with love. Are you getting the picture? Do you see how devastating saying "NO God" is?

Many of us will say "NO God" after putting little or no effort into getting to know Him. Some of us will say "NO God" after investing years in trying to get to know Him. Substituting rules, regulations, and rituals for a relationship. No matter what, we all get to make the same choice, and in the end, it all boils down to you either saying "YES God" or "NO God!" Again, this choice will always be yours to make. You just have to make sure you choose wisely.

God wants us to get to a point in our relationship with Him where we can say, "God, no matter what, I'm going to love You!"

Perspective #92: God, no matter what, I'm going to love You!

Loving God is not easy. What if God tests your love for Him? How will you respond? What if He takes your father home to be with

Him, and then two and a half months later, He takes your brother, and a month after that, he takes one of your best friends? Can and will you say, "God, no matter what, I'm going to love you!"

Of course, this is not a question I can answer for you; this is a question you and God have to work out together. But before I go, let me give you one more question. Do you love God enough to say, "My love for God is unconditional"?

Perspective #93: My love for God is unconditional!

Be careful. Think about this for a minute. Regardless of what God does, or allows to be done in your life, can and will you say, "My love for God is unconditional"? Here again, this is not a question I can answer for you; this is only something you can work out with Him. We always need to understand and remember Perspective #10: "Just because things are not going the way you planned doesn't mean they are not going the way they should."

This requires you to trust God for every aspect of your life: good, bad and ugly! This isn't easy. I know it hasn't been easy for me, Mr. Temper-Tantrum! So many times, in my past, when God has challenged me, I have gotten angry and thrown a temper-tantrum. My desire is never to do that again. I truly want to say, "God, no matter what, I'm going to love you!" After all, no matter what, God loves me! And no matter what, God loves you, even if you don't love Him. Even if you don't love you, He still does!

Perspective #94: No matter what, God loves you,
even if you don't love Him. Even if you don't love
you, He still does!

A few years ago, at work, I was having a horrible day. It was the day I went from hero to zero. After three years of doing everything I could to help this company succeed, I got told 25 different things I was doing wrong. My boss had a bulleted list, and he went through every one of them and wanted me to sign the list and promise to rectify them.

If you've ever come in early, stayed late and worked your butt off to make a difference only to be told it's not good enough, you know what

I mean. Devastated, I left the office right after that. I was supposed to meet my wife and daughter for dinner but could only seem to drive around in circles. I did not know how to face them in this condition. As I turned into the restaurant, I threw my hands up in frustration crying, "God, what else can I do? Nothing I do ever seems to be good enough." Finally, I had to pull over. At this point, I was on the verge of tears begging God, "Give me something, anything. I do not know what to do. I do not know how to respond." I don't know why but I turned on the car radio, and at that very moment, the song *No Matter What* by Kerrie Roberts came on. If you haven't listened to it, I highly recommend it; it is now one of my favorites. The start of the song goes something like this:

> I'm running back to your promises one more time
> Lord that's all I can hold on to
> I gotta say this has taken me by surprise
> But nothing surprises You
>
> Before a heartache can ever touch my life
> It has to go through Your hands
> And even though I keep asking why
> I keep asking why
>
> No matter what, I'm gonna love You
> No matter what I'm gonna need You
> I know You can find a way to keep me from the pain
> But if not, I'll trust you
> No matter what, no matter what

It's a choice to love God, no matter what. Me, I want to make that choice every second of every day. I'm not very good at it yet, but I'm hoping someday I will be.

Now you can see why I love this song. It speaks volumes to me. Thank you, Kerrie! No matter what I do, no matter what I've done, God is going to love me. And this is the perspective I need to have with my relationship with God. No matter what happens, no matter what God allows to happen, even if He chooses to give me two beautiful boys with special needs, I'm going to love Him, I'm going to trust Him, no matter what!

Let me encourage you to continue this journey with me in getting to know God and discovering who He is and what He's like. Pick up a copy of the next book in this series, or visit WalkerJamesAuthor.com to sign up for our newsletter, or to ask your questions and find valuable materials to assist you in investing and growing your relationship with Him.

God bless!

Perspective Recap:

- **Perspective #86:** We are all sinners, every single one of us. Can one sinner adequately judge or condemn another sinner?
- **Perspective #87:** If you know anything about sin, sin is what interferes with your relationship with God.
- **Perspective #88:** Our salvation is never about what we can do; it is and always has been about what God has already done!
- **Perspective #89:** Only within a relationship with God can you successfully focus on doing good and refrain from doing evil.
- **Perspective #90:** No matter what you do, say, think or don't do, God is ALWAYS going to love you! No matter what!
- **Perspective #91:** Understand, God is never going to like your sin, but He is always going to love you!
- **Perspective #92:** God, no matter what, I'm going to love You!
- **Perspective #93:** My love for God is unconditional!
- **Perspective #94:** No matter what, God loves you, even if you don't love Him. Even if you don't love you, He still does!

Coming Soon!

As I mentioned at the beginning of this book, this is a series of books. This book is just the beginning of the series. Let me encourage you to continue the journey and to fall more in love with God by getting to know more of who He is. The ten books in this series are:

Perspectives- Book 1: What Does God Want?

Perspectives-Book 2: The Power of Choice

Perspectives-Book 3: Is the Bible the Word of God?

Perspectives-Book 4: Grasping the Trinity

Perspectives-Book 5: Knowing God the Father

Perspectives-Book 6: Knowing God the Son

Perspectives-Book 7: Knowing God the Holy Spirit

Perspectives-Book 8: Knowing Your Enemy

Perspectives-Book 9: Investing in Your Relationship with God

Perspectives-Book 10: Living Your Relationship with God

Please look for these at your favorite eBook retailer, online bookstore, audio bookstore, and local bookstore.

I would love to hear how God is making an impact in your life or about any questions or concerns you may still have. Please feel free to visit my website WalkerJamesAuthor.com, you can reach out to me from there.

My warmest blessings!

Walker

Appendix A – Prayer of Salvation

A relationship with God begins when you recognize you are a sinner who has disobeyed God and His commands. You desire to surrender to God and fall into His love, mercy, and grace. You desire to repent (turn away from) these sins and enter a close, personal, loving, intimate, relationship with God the Father, through faith in His Beloved Son Jesus Christ, by the power of the Holy Spirit.

This is the only way to enter a relationship with God. All sin must be judged and punished. You can either choose to accept the punishment for yourself or choose by faith to accept Jesus as your Lord and Savior. He has already been judged and punished for your sin even though He was completely innocent of all sin!

To do this, simply pray this prayer with an open heart, an open mind, and a sincere desire for a relationship with God.

Father God, I humble myself before you and surrender to you repenting of my sins and telling you I'm sorry for all the terrible things I've done, the sins I've committed. I ask that You forgive me of these sins and cleanse me from my unrighteousness. By faith, I accept Your Son Jesus Christ into my heart and my life; I freely open the gift you have given me through Your Son Jesus Christ. Fill me with Your Spirit that I might be a beautiful reflection of Your Son Jesus. Help me from this day forward to love You, honor You and serve You, to shine You, Your light and Your love into other people's lives. Thank You for loving me so much to send Your Son Jesus to die for my sins. Help me to live the rest of my life for You and Your glory. Help me to always be about investing in my relationship with You! In the precious name of Your Son Jesus, I pray, Amen!

If you prayed this prayer, let me be the first to welcome you into the Kingdom of God!

Remember, God wants a relationship with you, and like any good relationship, you get out of it what you put into it. Spend time with Him in prayer every day, talk to Him like you would talk to a friend or a loved one. Read the Bible daily to learn more about Him and what He's like. Get connected with a good church that preaches the Word of God. Also, continue reading this series as it is designed with you in mind. It will take you through the journey of getting to know God, who He is and what He's like. If you'd like more information on how to do this best, just let me know. I'd love to help.

You can let me know of your decision, watch videos of other subjects, download the next eBook or purchase an audiobook by visiting our website at WalkerJamesAuthor.com.

Appendix B – Summary of Perspectives

The following is a list of the Perspectives I've put forth in this book. I've added the page # for where they can be found in this book, so you can easily go back and reference the discussion.

- **Perspective #1**: Your perspective of God is irrelevant compared to God's perspective of Himself! (Page 8)
- **Perspective #2:** Be patient. God's Word is essential to getting to know Him. Do not skip it, and do not ignore it. Respect it, and it will teach you great and wonderful things about Him! (Page 10)
- **Perspective #3:** Your relationship with God is a journey. Over time, as you partner with Him and cooperate with Him, He molds and shapes you into a beautiful reflection of His Son Jesus Christ. (Page 11)
- **Perspective #4:** God doesn't have to defend Himself, especially to you. After all, He is God and you are not. (Page 18)
- **Perspective #5:** Asking God the WHY question is usually asking for the silent treatment. Because He is God, He doesn't owe anyone an answer to WHY! (Page 18)
- **Perspective #6:** "EVERYTHING that comes into your life must FIRST go through the hands of God." – Greg Laurie (Page 19)
- **Perspective #7:** If we never take the time to learn from our trials, how can God get any value out of them and use us to give the lesson and the love to someone else? (Page 20)
- **Perspective #8:** Knowing that God wants to spend time with us should encourage us to want to spend time with Him! (Page 21)
- **Perspective #9:** When we look at our lives from God's perspective, we can then cooperate with Him, partner with Him and His plan for His Kingdom! (Page 21)
- **Perspective #10:** Just because things are not going the way we planned doesn't mean they are not going the way they should! – Christine Caine (Page 22)
- **Perspective #11:** Your perspective has a direct impact on the depth and quality of your life. Choose a negative perspective and get negative results. Choose a positive perspective and get positive results. (Page 22)

- **Perspective #12:** That is what God's love does! He cares for you even when you don't care for Him. (Page 23)
- **Perspective #13:** How much evidence will it take for you to believe that God does indeed exist? That God does indeed love and care for you deeply? (Page 25)
- **Perspective #14:** Truth can be hard to find and hard to uncover. (Page 25)
- **Perspective #15:** Truth will always reward the diligent who sincerely seek after her and are not afraid of her. (Page 25)
- **Perspective #16:** God will hold you accountable for all the evidence of His existence, regardless of whether you believe it or not. (Page 27 and 36)
- **Perspective #17:** "The finite (limited) cannot prove or disprove the existence of the infinite (unlimited)." – Skip Heitzig (Page 30)
- **Perspective #18:** Just because you can't see God doesn't mean He doesn't exist. (Page 32)
- **Perspective #19:** If something has design, it MUST have a designer. (Page 32)
- **Perspective #20:** DNA proves we have design. Code, blueprints, and instruction manuals do not write themselves. When you have design, you MUST have a designer! (Page 33)
- **Perspective #21:** To put a copy of how to make something in every cell of that something so that every cell carries the instructions of how to make that something is pure genius! (Page 34)
- **Perspective #22:** We are not an accident. When you have a clear and deliberate design, you eliminate accidents and instead, you have purpose. (Page 34)
- **Perspective #23:** God doesn't need you to believe in Him for Him to exist. (Page 35)
- **Perspective #24:** God doesn't need your permission to exist. (Page 35)
- **Perspective #25:** You ARE accountable to God, regardless of what you believe! (Page 35)

- **Perspective #26:** "'If God is NOT an integral part of your life equation, you WILL end up with the wrong answer." – Valerie Knox (Page 36)
- **Perspective #27:** Life is extremely complicated. If you leave God out of your life equation, you will end up with the wrong answer. You are missing THE key variable to solving the equation to life. (Page 38)
- **Perspective #28:** Without God in your life, life for you is not what He created it to be. (Page 37)
- **Perspective #29:** God wants a close, personal, loving, intimate relationship with you! (Page 40)
- **Perspective #30:** Jesus Christ is the bath you need to take to be cleansed of all your sin—past, present, and future! (Page 42)
- **Perspective #31:** God has prepared the bath (Jesus Christ) you need to take to cleanse you from the dirt of your sin. All you need to do is agree to take the bath! (Page 42)
- **Perspective #32:** This perspective that God wants a relationship with you is critical if you want to get to know Him, love Him, serve Him, cooperate with Him, and partner with Him in what He's doing in His Kingdom. (Page 45)
- **Perspective #33:** God wants peace with you. He wants to be friends. (Page 45)
- **Perspective #34:** God wants you to know Him, which means God is knowable! (Page 46)
- **Perspective #35:** To have a relationship with God, you must first surrender your life to Him. (Page 46)
- **Perspective #36:** God's conditions for a relationship with Him are surrender—complete, absolute, and total surrender! (Page 47)
- **Perspective #37:** God does not want a relationship with you through a third party. He wants a relationship with YOU personally! (Page 48)
- **Perspective #38:** To "know" God requires an investment in the time it takes to get to know Him. (Page 50)
- **Perspective #39:** "God is NEVER an intruder in our lives – He is only an invited guest." – Michael Franzese (Page 50)

- **Perspective #40:** Understand that a relationship with God means you desire to get to know Him and who He is. You want to honor Him in everything you do, say and think. (Page 52)
- **Perspective #41:** A relationship with God is choosing to fall in love with Him. It is choosing to be grateful for Him and for what He's done for you. (Page 53)
- **Perspective #42:** You have the EXACT relationship with God YOU want! (Page 53)
- **Perspective #43:** Your level of intimacy with God, your level of friendship with God, your level of partnership and cooperation with God, and your level of love for God are all under your power and control! (Page 53)
- **Perspective #44:** If you can have as much of God as you want, how much of God will you take? (Page 54)
- **Perspective #45:** Jesus wants us to get rid of all the other distractions, all the other things in our lives that interfere with our relationship with Him! (Page 55)
- **Perspective #46:** God is NEVER afraid of your questions! (Page 58)
- **Perspective #47:** The only difference between success and failure is "success" NEVER gives up! (Page 58)
- **Perspective #48:** There is a fine line that separates those who are successful in this world from those who are failures. This line of separation is perseverance. Successful people never give up. (Page 59)
- **Perspective #49:** God doesn't owe anyone an answer to a "why" question! (Page 61)
- **Perspective #50:** Questions challenge and validate our thinking, allowing us to go through the process of justifying what we believe and why. (Page 62)
- **Perspective #51:** Even though it may be difficult to do, we must always remove any obstacle to our relationship with God. (Page 66)
- **Perspective #52:** "Never argue with a fool in public. Nobody knows who the fool is!" – Maureen Rose Plein (Page 71)

- **Perspective #53:** "Never argue with a fool in public. They will drag you down to their level and then beat you with experience." – Mark Twain (Page 71)
- **Perspective #54:** God will not hold you accountable for what someone else says about Him; He will only hold you accountable for what you believe is true. (Page 72)
- **Perspective #55:** God is excited to teach you, to grow you and to guide you! His passion and His desire is to help you fall more in love with Him and with who He is! (Page 72)
- **Perspective #56:** How you respond to God and to His truth has everything to do with your relationship with Him. (Page 75)
- **Perspective #57:** God can see our hearts and our motives. If we come to Him with a sincere heart, He will go out of His way to answer our questions. (Page 76)
- **Perspective #58:** God is not a genie in a bottle who will perform for you anytime you demand it as if you can "make" Him do something. (Page 77)
- **Perspective #59:** Because He is all-powerful, God can and will make everyone stand before Him and give an account of their life. (Page 77)
- **Perspective #60:** Because He is all-powerful, God doesn't have to prove Himself on demand for your amusement! (Page 78)
- **Perspective #61:** We have been designed by God to learn, grow, and discover all the intricate things about Him and His creation that He has made available to us. (Page 81)
- **Perspective #62:** Learning is a lifelong process of growing in our relationship with God, cooperating with Him, and partnering with Him! (Page 82)
- **Perspective #63:** Failures are the stepping stones to success! Do not waste the failure; learn from it, grow from it, and use it to become a success! (Page 82)
- **Perspective #64:** The only way to truly fail is to give up and quit—to throw your toys out the window and walk off the playing field! (Page 83)
- **Perspective #65:** Do not focus on what you don't know about God; instead, focus on what you DO know about God. (Page 84)

- **Perspective #66:** Embrace what you do know about God and quit dwelling on what you don't know. (Page 84)
- **Perspective #67:** We have a BIG God and small minds; we are not capable of knowing everything there is to know about God. (Page 85)
- **Perspective #68:** Success is a process of repeated learning (a.k.a. failure) until you get it right. (Page 85)
- **Perspective #69:** Be sure to always compare what other people say to what the Bible says about God; that way, you will always be able to discern His truth! (Page 88)
- **Perspective #70:** Since God wants a close, personal, loving, intimate relationship with you, then He positively wants you to ASK Him everything. (Page 88)
- **Perspective #71:** Your sincere questions only stoke the fires of your learning engine and can only enhance and grow your relationship with God. (Page 89)
- **Perspective #72:** Faith is your link to God, your umbilical cord with God, so to speak, where He can empower you with His wisdom and grace. (Page 92)
- **Perspective #73:** You will become what you focus on. (Page 93)
- **Perspective #74:** Your freedom, your ransom, and your redemption from sin and death cost God everything. He gave His most precious gift, His most valued possession to save you! (Page 98)
- **Perspective #75:** Jesus Christ GAVE Himself freely, paid the price FULLY, for ALL who accept His gift of love! You, me, everyone! (Page 99)
- **Perspective #76:** God spared no expense to redeem you from sin and death. (Page 99)
- **Perspective #77:** If God spared no expense to ransom you and to redeem you, what does that say about how valuable and precious you are to God? (Page 99)
- **Perspective #78:** If you have accepted Jesus as your Lord and Savior, you are a valuable, precious, pure, spotless, holy, beautiful prince or princess of the most high God! (Page 101)

- **Perspective #79:** You are not an accident; you are not a mistake. Even if someone has told you this before or said they never wanted you, be assured, God has always wanted you. (Page 101)
- **Perspective #80:** Jesus did not want to live in heaven without you, which is why He "chose" to die for you so that you could spend eternity with Him! (Page 101)
- **Perspective #81:** "God's love for you does not have a beginning; it never started. He has always loved you!" – Brad Camp (Page 103)
- **Perspective #82:** "What other people think about you is NONE of YOUR business. Focus on what God thinks about you and your relationship with Him. That is YOUR business." – Pastor Ron Wood (Page 103)
- **Perspective #83:** The question you need to ask anyone who discourages you from pursuing a relationship with God is, "How far would you go to have a relationship with me? Would you go as far as God went?" (Page 103)
- **Perspective #84:** God didn't HAVE to do what He did, but because of your need and my need, He chose to do it. (Page 104)
- **Perspective #85:** Even though God doesn't need a relationship with you, He wants a relationship with you. (Page 104)
- **Perspective #86:** We are all sinners, every single one of us. Can one sinner adequately judge or condemn another sinner? (Page 109)
- **Perspective #87:** If you know anything about sin, sin is what interferes with your relationship with God (Page 109)
- **Perspective #88:** Our salvation is never about what we can do; it is and always has been about what God has already done! (Page 110)
- **Perspective #89:** Only within a relationship with God can you successfully focus on doing good and refrain from doing evil. (Page 110)
- **Perspective #90:** No matter what you do, say, think or don't do, God is ALWAYS going to love you! No matter what! (Page 111)
- **Perspective #91:** Understand, God is never going to like your sin, but He is always going to love you! (Page 111)

Made in the USA
Middletown, DE
30 September 2018